YOU CAN CHANGE THE WORLD

It was a special grace to read Archbishop John Foley's Foreword to this new edition of Fr. James Keller's *You Can Change the World*. My own recollection of Fr. Keller was an interview that he was kind enough to give me in the 1950's when Archbishop John J. Maguire, then Coadjutor Archbishop of New York, sent me to meet him and to find out from him how he thought a young priest of New York could be useful in somehow helping "to change the world." I will never forget that interview, although it is almost 50 years ago. His graciousness in giving me the time, his thoughtfulness in providing me with a glimpse of his own great vision and his encouragement were unforgettable elements of a great half hour in my life. I am so pleased that Alba House is making it possible for a new generation to read the book that truly helped change the world because it helped so many people know that they could have a role in that great enterprise. Fr. Keller writes with clarity, with affection and with deep faith. I welcome this new Anniversary Edition and hope that it can be put into the hands of millions of people who need to be reminded of the role that they can play in making this tired, old world of ours come alive with love again.

Cardinal Theodore McCarrick
Archbishop of Washington

A couple of years ago Jerry Costello and I were talking about Father Keller's best-selling book, *You Can Change the World*, and we agreed that with some modest updating, the spirit of what Father Keller wrote in 1948 would still be perfectly appropriate today. Jerry took on the task of revising the book, and has done an excellent job of keeping the truth and wisdom of the challenge Father Keller made to us nearly sixty years ago.

The original message of *You Can Change the World* applies just as much today as it did then. Each of us has the God-given talents and abilities to change the world. Father Keller encourages us to take the steps that will make a positive difference in our lives and in our world.

An entire generation enjoyed and profited from Father Keller's book when it first appeared. Now, with the release of this Anniversary Edition, today's readers can do exactly the same.

Dennis W. Heaney, President
The Christophers

You Can Change the World made me believe that I could somehow be a force for good when I was still a teenager. Father Keller inspired me to think big as television flowered in the early 50's, and dare to dream that I might find a way of using television to help inform and educate people. Father Keller and The Christophers have influenced generations of young people to believe they could make a difference. I am thrilled to see the Anniversary Edition of his book which I believe will continue to infuse readers with a sense of purpose and with the idealism that Father Keller so passionately intended and so forcefully taught.

Joan Ganz Cooney
Co-founder, Sesame Workshop
Creator of *Sesame Street*

Father James Keller's

YOU CAN
CHANGE
THE
WORLD

ANNIVERSARY EDITION

Edited and Abridged
with a New Introduction by Gerald M. Costello

The Christophers
www.christophers.org

Alba
House

Library of Congress Cataloging-in-Publication Data

Keller, James, 1900-1977.
　　　[You can change the world]
　　　Father James Keller's You can change the world / edited and abridged with a
new introduction by Gerald M. Costello. — Anniversary ed.
　　　p. cm.
　　　Includes bibliographical references.
　　　ISBN 0-8189-1234-0
　　　1. Christian life—Catholic authors. 2. Christian life—United States.
3. Christophers (Organization)　I. Costello, Gerald M.　II. Title.

BX2350.3.K44 2006
248.4'82—dc22

　　　　　　　　　　　　　　　　2006004781

Scripture passages are from the Revised Standard Version of the Bible,
New Testament Section, Copyright 1946, by Division of Christian Education of
the National Council of the Churches of Christ in the United States of America.

Produced and designed in the United States of America by the
Fathers and Brothers of the Society of St. Paul,
2187 Victory Boulevard, Staten Island, New York 10314-6603,
as part of their communications apostolate.

ISBN: 0-8189-1234-0
ISBN: 978-0-8189-1234-4

Printing Information:

Current Printing - first digit	1	2	3	4	5	6	7	8	9	10

Year of Current Printing - first year shown

2006	2007	2008	2009	2010	2011	2012	2013	2014	2015

Table of Contents

Editor's Acknowledgments and Notes

I wasn't aware of it at the time, but this book began to develop almost from the moment I arrived at The Christophers in 2000. As a member of the organization's Board of Directors who was retired from full time employment, I had been asked to serve as Interim Administrator of The Christophers and to head the Search Committee looking for a new priest-director. It was an assignment that I expected might last six months. With a succession of titles that would include that of President, however, it wound up taking me nearly three years.

During that time my chief associate was Mary Ellen Robinson, then Executive Assistant to the Director. From the start her assistance, counsel and friendship proved invaluable. From the start, too, she encouraged me to use my writing experience to promote in some way the good work done every day by priests all over the world — the kind of work too often forgotten amid the sensationalized reporting of clerical scandals involving a very, very few. Among the priests she cited as worthy of further attention was Maryknoll Father James Keller, founder of The Christophers. His name came forward ever more often as we worked together to plan a centennial birthday celebration in Father Keller's memory in December, 2000. His writings had inspired her and countless others to follow the Christopher path, she said; perhaps they could be updated for today's readers.

The idea remained alive but never got beyond the talking stage — not, at any rate, until the arrival of the new President of The Christophers: Dennis Heaney, the first lay person to serve permanently as the organization's chief executive officer. Our Search Committee had labored long and hard to find a priest who would continue as Director in the Christopher tradition, but the pool of available priests had shrunk dramatically. Once the Board determined that a lay person might be designated for the post, it took the Search Committee not long at all to choose Dennis.

A veteran of the Catholic press, he came to The Christophers from *The Tidings,* the Los Angeles archdiocesan newspaper, where he had served as executive publisher. For several years before that he held a similar position at *The Catholic Spirit,* newspaper of the St. Paul-Minneapolis Archdiocese. He was also a long-time friend, blessed with superior professional talents and admirable personal traits. Dennis put his broad communications abilities to good use at The Christophers, where he soon discovered that the name of James Keller still held a magic appeal to thousands of Christopher friends. With that in mind, early in 2005 he invited me to help celebrate the 60th anniversary of The Christophers by editing, updating and writing a new introduction for *You Can Change the World,* Father Keller's best-known (and best-selling) book. The idea struck me as perfect — not only as an ideal way to mark the occasion, but also to acquaint modern-day readers with the vision that was Father Keller's.

Without Mary Ellen's initial prompting and Dennis' specific invitation, then, this Anniversary Edition of *You Can Change the World* might never have appeared. I am immensely grateful to them both.

Others must be thanked as well:

Archbishop John P. Foley, President of the Vatican's Pontifical Commission for Social Communications (who himself was inspired as a student by Father Keller), for contributing the Foreword.

The Board of Directors of The Christophers, for endorsing this project so enthusiastically. The late Richard Armstrong, a former Director of The Christophers, whose biography of Father Keller, *Out to Change the World*, is rich with insights about his mentor and friend. Stephanie Raha, editor-in-chief of The Christophers, for helpful comments and suggestions. And my wife, Jane, the first editor of so much of the material that I write, whose observations are invariably right on the mark.

Notes

Editing and revising a classic work is a daunting task, made all the more so in this case by the legendary status of its author. The basic decisions that came from our earliest editorial conferences kept that in mind: use Father Keller's original text wherever possible, and use as much of it that remains timely and appropriate.

These are injunctions I have tried to follow throughout the book.

Father Keller wrote plainly and simply, in language that was easy to read and easy to understand. He had a message to get out, and he wanted as many readers as possible to know just what he meant. That's one reason his words stand up so well today. My alterations were few: changing a word every now and then (but not universally) to reflect a more advanced view of gender difference; eliminating some references to contemporary culture ("waiting for a streetcar") or figures, especially those relating to wages, that might prove distracting. For instance, referring to an "excellent salary" of $10,000 a year might have struck a resonant chord in 1948 — but not today.

Global events and the passage of time have left some of Father Keller's stories and examples out of date. That is particularly true of his repeated concern that Communists were working hard to "take over" institutions that were part of our way of life. Fortunately, because Keller illustrated the points he made with references to a great number of other topics, many of those involving the Communist threat of the 1940s could be dropped without impeding the book's narrative flow. Also, two brief chapters in the original *You Can Change the World*, those dealing with careers in the library field and in social work, are not included in this edition. This was done only because library and social service structures have changed so extensively that his descriptions of career opportunities available at the time no longer apply.

The world of labor-management relations has changed greatly as well. At a time of sharply declining numbers connected to organized labor and an increasing politicization within the field, it is hard to know how Father Keller would have regarded it today. It's safe to say, though, that his somewhat idealized view of both labor and management would be hard to recognize today.

Education in the United States has also changed mightily since Keller's time, although in this case it is much easier to assume what his reaction might have been. He wrote at a time when prayer was a daily part of public school life, and references to God were not only permitted but encouraged. That those things no longer hold would have appalled Father Keller, and they make his warnings about "godless elements" dictating a future agenda for American schools even more to the point.

James Keller, presumably, would have been sympathetic to efforts to update his presentation for readers of the future. In the chapter on "Speaking in Public" in this book, for example, he counseled maintaining an informal reference file on a number of likely speaking topics. But he also advised: "From time to time, run through your little collection of incidents or anecdotes, discarding those references which are no longer useful." Father Keller, consider that done.

What is most remarkable about *You Can Change the World,*

however, is not that change has been so all-encompassing that Keller's proposals seem hopelessly outdated today. Rather, it's that so many of the same problems remain, in one form or another, and that the way to start solving them is to follow the advice that Keller offered years ago — advice, in short, to become Christophers.

In his own words, once again, James Keller showed that in *You Can Change the World* he was looking far beyond the Communist menace to recognize and foresee the dangers that still confront us today. As he said:

> Communism and other evils may come and go, but this greater problem, involving a gradual loss of appreciation for the main foundations of our civilization, is far more serious than all of them put together. It is the heart of America's sickness today.

What a visionary he was. And what an honor it is for me to offer his words to a new generation.

About the Editor

Gerald M. Costello is a former President of The Christophers. A 1952 graduate of the University of Notre Dame, he was the founding editor of two Catholic newspapers: *The Beacon*, in Paterson, New Jersey, and *Catholic New York*. Now retired, he holds an honorary doctorate in letters from St. John's University, New York. The Catholic Press Association has presented him with both the St. Francis de Sales Award and the Bishop John England Award.

He and his wife, Jane, live in Pompton Plains, New Jersey. They have six children and sixteen grandchildren.

Also by Gerald M. Costello

Mission to Latin America: The Successes and Failures of a Twentieth-Century Crusade.

Without Fear or Favor: George Higgins on the Record.

Our Sunday Visitor's Treasury of Catholic Stories (Editor).

Foreword

By Archbishop John P. Foley
President, Pontifical Council for Social Communications

In 1948, I was a student in the eighth grade at Holy Spirit School in Sharon Hill, Pennsylvania, in the Archdiocese of Philadelphia — and, for my 13th birthday on November 11, or for Christmas (I can't remember which), my parents gave me the book *You Can Change the World* by Father James Keller, the founder of The Christophers. It was a book that changed my life — and theirs. The book advocated the choice of a career that could have an influence on society.

My father was already working for the Socony-Vacuum Oil Company (Mobil), but the Christopher idea led him to organize the Catholics in his company to make an annual spiritual retreat together and to become part of the Catholic Petroleum Guild, which had an annual Mass and Communion Breakfast and other activities in the Philadelphia area. He also became a candidate for the borough council in our little town (he lost), but all of his ideas in his campaign letters were put into practice by his incumbent opponents before the election — from filling the potholes in the streets to improving the street lighting. I told him he had actually won — without the inconvenience of having to go to meetings of the borough council!

My father was a great defender of workers, which probably cost him advancement in his career. But I still remember what he said: "Stockholders have invested their money, but employees have invested their lives" — a phrase on which many might meditate today. Although he was not even a high school graduate (although he was an avid reader), he went to the St. Joseph's College Institute of Industrial Relations and studied the papal social encyclicals so that he could do his own job better — and with a better spirit.

My mother was a housewife, but she became active in the Archbishop's Committee for Home and Family, a group that visited new mothers in the parish, distributing material on child rearing and the religious formation of children. When she encountered a family in which the mother did not speak English, my mother took courses in Spanish so that she might be able to communicate with the woman! My mother also became a volunteer at the Catholic Information Center of Philadelphia and she became president of the parents' organization at St. Joseph's College when I was a student there. After my ordination to the priesthood, she became president of the Priests' Mothers' Association and changed its name to the Priests' Parents' Association — asking why the organization should discriminate against men!

My mother and father and I (I was an only child) often spoke of The Christophers at dinner time — and we were all faithful readers of Christopher News Notes, and The Christophers received at least annual donations from my parents, who were great fans of the organization and its ideals.

I have spoken of the influence of The Christophers on my parents.

Regarding the influence of *You Can Change the World* on my own life, Father Keller had spoken of the importance of careers in politics, education, communications and labor relations. Since I followed radio drama with great interest (this was before the days of the dominance of television), I took my cue from Father Keller and got books from the library on how to write radio plays — and I began to write plays on the lives of the saints, since I thought that people would benefit from good role models.

By the time I entered high school (St. Joseph's Prep, the Jesuit school in Philadelphia), I had finished several scripts, and I took them to the student counselor who put me in contact with the priest-director of radio and television in the Archdiocese, who in turn put me in contact with a woman who worked at WCAU, the CBS station in Philadelphia. Her name was Margaret Mary Kearney, and she had long worked in the archdiocesan school system, coaching speech. She was very generous in helping me with scripts, and she contacted the owner of a small radio station, WJMJ ("1540, top of the dial and clear as a bell in Philadelphia"), who read the scripts and invited me and several other students from St. Joseph's to produce them on his radio station. He then asked me if I was interested in becoming a volunteer announcer for Catholic radio programming on Sunday mornings on the station. So, beginning at the age of 14, I became a radio announcer.

Also at St. Joseph's Prep, with the encouragement of my eighth-grade teacher, Mother Mary Berchmans (now Sister Elizabeth Gorvin), of the Society of the Holy Child Jesus, the best teacher I ever had, I became involved in teaching religion to orphans from Girard College, the special school founded by Revolutionary War financier Stephen Girard, who forbade access to his school by ministers of any religion. Thus, I became active in another field recommended by Father Keller, education!

Later, at St. Joseph's University, I became involved in television — in a program called "Debate" on the local NBC station, which was experimenting with color in 1954. I also had the opportunity to produce several programs about Catholic education on a local independent station. In all of this, my motivation was "to light one candle" — in keeping with the motto of Father Keller.

While at St. Joseph's University, as members of the Sodality, several of us visited local drug stores to get Christopher books (including *You Can Change the World*) onto the paperback book racks — and then we convinced some people to go into the stores and ask for them, so that we could get the drug stores to restock them!

In my part-time job as a university student, I had to become a member of a labor union, the Teamsters — and so I went to the union meeting, an action also recommended by Father Keller, but my suggestions at the meeting were greeted by an invitation by several muscular men to leave the meeting and never return! I quit the job and got another.

After graduating from college, I entered the seminary, convinced that, for me, the best way to become a Christopher, a "Christ-bearer," was to accept the invitation to become a priest, "another Christ." I have often said that I have never had an unhappy day as a priest, and I think that part of the reason for that, by God's grace, has been the positive attitude stressed by the late Father Keller — to light a candle and not to curse the darkness, to affirm the good and to encourage the struggling, to change the world for the better, one action at a time, one step after another.

More than 50 years ago, Father Keller convinced my parents and myself that we could change the world — and we all tried! I encourage those who read this new edition of *You Can Change the World* to be Christophers, to be "Christ-bearers." As the late Pope John Paul II said in 1978 in the inaugural Mass of his papacy, "Be not afraid!"

"Be not afraid!" — "You can change the world!"

General Introduction

The Priest

"James Keller, Missionary."

That's not the wording on his tombstone, nor was it the headline over his obituary when Father James Keller, M.M., died in 1977. But those who knew him say he would have enjoyed that thumbnail description as much as any. He saw himself as a missionary first and foremost, and felt sure that ultimately his missioner's zeal was behind all he accomplished in life.

Mission was in James Keller's veins. It steered him to ordination as a priest of Maryknoll, the society that sent Americans to the missions overseas. It guided him on his travels to the Far East, and inspired his tireless fund-raising and speaking on behalf of Maryknoll. It motivated his work as an official of the Society for the Propagation of the Faith, which allocates funds to foreign mission efforts, and as editor of Maryknoll's mission magazine. It came to full flower in his role as founder of The Christophers, a missionary movement unlike any other.

In his 1963 autobiography, *To Light a Candle*, Keller explained that he deliberately kept The Christophers simple and uncomplicated in its organization, leaving each individual Christopher able to focus on the specific God-given mission that he or she would first discern and then fulfill. As he wrote:

I have tried never to lose sight of what I regarded as the big objective behind the Christopher idea: to make every person a missioner.

James Keller was born in Oakland, California, in 1900, a date that would underscore his role as quintessentially a man of the twentieth century. His father had his own haberdashery store, and the large Keller family — two girls and four boys — led a pleasant middle-class life. There was Mass every Sunday to attend, but no particular religious fervor in the Keller household — which reacted with some surprise when young James entered St. Patrick's Seminary in Menlo Park, at the tender age of 14, to begin studies for the diocesan priesthood.

He stayed for three years before encountering some doubts and dropped out for a while to help run a candy store and soda fountain owned by his uncles. It was there, just outside the store, that Keller, then all of 17, ran into a young priest and had a conversation that would change his life. When Keller mentioned his doubts about going back to the seminary, the priest said he would never advise him not to return. "After all," he continued, "in God's plan there may be thousands of people whose salvation depends on what you may do for them as a priest."

The priest's words left a permanent imprint on Keller's heart. So did visits to St. Patrick's (where Keller returned to continue his priestly studies) by missioners of the still-new Maryknoll community. "I was deeply impressed by the forthright manner of these frontier-breaking men of God," he wrote. "The missionary side of the Church suddenly took on a new and deeper meaning." James Keller resolved to make that meaning his own, and with the permission of his religious superiors and the approval of Maryknoll, took his first train trip East and enrolled at the mission organization's seminary in 1921.

He took to it from the start, and after some additional studies at the Catholic University of America was ordained a Maryknoll priest in 1925. His first assignment was something of a disappointment; instead of going off to the missions he'd be doing promotion work for Maryknoll in California — "not in the mission fields as I had hoped, but at least working *for* them."

No one who knew Jim Keller would be surprised that he turned in an outstanding performance as motivational speaker, fund-raiser, and developer of Maryknoll vocations — so much so that he was rewarded with a first-hand look at the missions in 1928 on a tour of Australia, the Dutch East Indies, China, Korea and Japan.

That trip not only gave him his first experience with the inroads being made by Communists overseas — "on a frightening scale," he would later write — but also helped prepare him for an enhanced role as Maryknoll's chief promoter and developer, based in New York. From 1934 to 1937 he was also assistant director of the Society for the Propagation of the Faith, breathing new life into that office, but he eventually gave that up because of his Maryknoll responsibilities. His gifts extended into the field of magazine editing; he revitalized both *Catholic Missions,* for the Propagation of the Faith, and *The Field Afar,* Maryknoll's popular mission journal.

Not only did Keller become an increasingly familiar figure throughout the Northeast, where his speaking engagements went on virtually non-stop, but he also turned his hand to writing. With the help of a legendary *New York Times* reporter named Meyer Berger he produced his first book, *Men of Maryknoll* (based primarily on tales he heard from returning missioners). A more reflective article — "What About the Hundred Million?" — appeared in the *American Ecclesiastical Review* in 1945. Like so much that Keller did, the article — which called for Catholics to reach out in a special way to their many fellow Americans who had no church ties at all — caused a sensation, touching off a wave of interest in the idea and in the man behind it.

In the meantime, the thoughts behind the movement that

would be known as The Christophers began to coalesce. They focused on the need for an individual concept of mission, and they were first developed most identifiably in a talk Keller gave at the Convent of the Sacred Heart in Noroton, Connecticut, in the 1930s. He told the young women students there that each of them could personally do something, with the help of Jesus, to change the world for the better, adding that they could become "Christophers" — Christbearers — in the process.

"How I happened to use that word at that particular time I don't know," Father Keller wrote in his autobiography. "To the best of my recollection I had never used it in that way before. But having done so, I felt that here, at last, was the root of the idea that had been in my mind for so long."

Father Keller's schedule was clearly a full one, but by the mid-1940s the organization that would be known as The Christophers was calling more and more for his time. Although he traced its formal founding to 1945, the birth was more gradual than dramatic.

Maryknoll, of course, was reluctant to see him go. As the religious community's chief promoter and spokesman, he had increased its visibility — and, not coincidentally, its treasury as well. Some Maryknollers even suggested that a mission assignment would help Keller get over his preoccupation with the Christopher idea. But by this time the dynamic priest was not to be deterred. He wanted to devote all his time to The Christophers, even offering to withdraw from Maryknoll if that's what it would take.

Then, in 1946, came a Maryknoll General Chapter — a major policy-and-planning session, along with the election of new leaders — that would help to settle the issue. A new superior general, reversing a previous course, encouraged Keller to continue with the development of The Christophers. That same year Keller's "You Can Be a Christopher" article appeared in *The Catholic World,* setting off another wave of enthusiasm. From that point on, The Christophers were more or less on their own.

The 1948 publication of *You Can Change the World* would help launch the organization into a period of explosive growth. So would Keller's friendship with the era's rich and famous (especially those who were Catholic), the movers and shakers whose endorsement gave the priest constant exposure in the press and among those who shaped the opinions of others. "His mission assignment," commented Richard Armstrong, Keller's successor as director of The Christophers and later his biographer, "took him among the influential in America."

Indeed it did. He was at home with Mr. and Mrs. J. Peter Grace, with the McDonnells and the Fords, and even, at Hyannisport, with the Kennedys. "Had a long talk with Jack Kennedy," Keller wrote after a visit in 1940, when Kennedy was 23. "He is a lad who has a great future."

But Keller also appealed to the masses. As The Christophers grew in influence, with ever-expanding public support, so did its operations — News Notes, a book series called *Three Minutes a Day*, a daily newspaper column with the same title, movies (with Hollywood's leading stars), radio and television programs, and the Christopher Awards, which honored positive contributions from the creative and artistic community rather than carping about the negative. Christopher Career Institutes, which later evolved into the Christopher Leadership Course, steered graduates into influential careers and roles of leadership.

The Christophers grew, and so did Father Keller. He sustained a positive image in part because he steered clear of partisan politics (unlike another well-known priest-communicator of the time, Father Charles Coughlin). In fact, he generally avoided controversy of any kind — for one reason, according to Richard Armstrong, because "he knew his limitations."

Along with Monsignor (later Archbishop) Fulton J. Sheen, he was the best-known priest of his day. Entertainment figures who were otherwise reluctant to volunteer for public-interest projects were all too willing to pitch in for The Christophers. "I got involved," one of them said, "because Father Keller asked."

He could be a demanding taskmaster, perhaps because he himself worked so hard. His writing output alone was remarkable, his energy almost inexhaustible. To his staff, Armstrong wrote, Keller was something of a father figure, treating his employees "about the same way he treated his own family — amiably, but at arm's length."

Father Keller found it increasingly difficult to keep up with all the changes taking place, both in the Church and in society at large, during the 1960s. He was "basically a conservative man," Armstrong said — a reformer, but a gradual one. He was "stunned" by changes in Church practice spawned by Vatican Council II, but did his best to accept them graciously and eventually came to feel at home with them. Still, "He wondered where it would all lead," said Armstrong. To one friend he confessed that he hoped he would die "while he could still die a Catholic!"

But even as the years went by, Keller never stopped trying to change the world. And when he retired — in 1969, a year ahead of his own schedule, due to the advances of Parkinson's Disease, and eight years before his death — he could look back on a career of rich promise that had been gloriously fulfilled.

Keller summed up some of his thoughts on that point on the closing pages of his autobiography. He spoke of the "simple idea" behind The Christophers — that everyone, without exception, should have a mission, and work hard to integrate Gospel principles into every aspect of life.

"I never dreamed that I would be spending most of my priestly life trying to reach anyone and everyone with its possibilities from an office in the heart of Manhattan," he wrote. "Nor did I have even the vaguest notion that my own life would be so fully enriched in the process...."

"What has been accomplished thus far by this 'everyone can be a missioner' idea is only the beginning. It is just a slight preview of the hopeful transformation that can take place both here and throughout the world once enough people are captivated by the conviction that they can 'light a candle' instead of 'curse the darkness'."

The Book

You Can Change the World was first published in 1948, and by anyone's definition it was a blockbuster from the start.

For one thing, it made its appearance in the book world at just the right time. The euphoria that had marked the end of World War II three years earlier was fast dissipating, and fear of what lay ahead — the possibility of atomic conflict and the looming menace of global Communism — was just as quickly taking its place. In *You Can Change the World* Father James Keller confronted those fears for his readers, asserting strongly that the best strategy to overcome them combined traditional American values with a living faith in Jesus Christ.

Then too, Father Keller was already well on his way to a degree of recognition by the general public. In an era when both the media and society at large looked up to the priesthood with an admiration that bordered on reverence, this was critical to the book's success. Further, the loosely knit organization he had founded, The Christophers, was becoming familiar to the nation. People wanted to know what was behind The Christophers, what the organization was all about.

Finally, Keller wrote with a straightforward style that readers liked. There was nothing fancy about it; just a plain way of talking to people that told them yes, they had cause to be concerned, but at the same time assured them they could do something about it.

No wonder *You Can Change the World* sold 250,000 copies in hardcover and another 300,000 in paperback. No wonder it was condensed in the *Reader's Digest*, a tribute to its bestseller status.

No wonder it was turned into a movie seen by audiences from coast to coast, with a cast of stars that included Bob Hope and Bing Crosby. And no wonder people who read the book believed Keller when he told them they could change the world. Many of them went out and did just that.

Father Keller had written other books before *You Can Change the World*, and they enjoyed at least a modest success. But most were addressed directly to priests or to Father Keller's fellow Catholics. Despite its obvious grounding in Christianity in general and Catholicism in particular, this one reached out to everybody. The heart of its message was clear: godless Communism presents a real threat to the nation and to the world, but the danger can be overcome if people of good will work together positively and stand up for what is right.

Not coincidentally, it also set forth the philosophical underpinnings of The Christophers.

"It is much more than the dollars, food, medicine and material things of America that the world needs and really wants," Keller wrote. "What they crave, above all else, is the spirit that makes America the great nation it is. And that spirit, above all else, is God's truth proclaiming through the Declaration of Independence, the Constitution, and the Bill of Rights that even the least individual as a child of God has rights that no man or nation can take from him — the right to life, to liberty, and to the pursuit of happiness which begins here, but which will have its supreme fulfillment in eternity."

Father Keller recycled some earlier material for parts of *You Can Change the World*, including sections taken from his first few Christopher News Notes and other bits and pieces tucked away in his files. He started putting the pages together in 1947 and completed the work the following summer, with a newspaperman named Charles Oxton providing a hand with editing and rewriting. Among those who checked the manuscript was Fulton Oursler, senior editor of the *Reader's Digest* and a friend of Keller's.

As it turned out, Oursler would make a key contribution. Looking over the typewritten pages, he came across a phrase that jumped out at him — so much so that he suggested it for the book's title. It proved to be the happiest of choices. *You Can Change the World* was more than a challenging, dynamic title; it remains The Christophers' key message to this day.

Thanks in part to Father Keller's growing popularity, the book debuted with a splash. Leading publications were quick to take notice, and critics generally liked what they saw. *The Saturday Review of Literature*, for example, even though it perceived something "amateurish" in the work and found a bit of repetition on its pages, correctly gauged the book's potential. "...It has something which can make it an epic — a simple, explosive, contagious idea," the review read. "And, if ideas are important as we have been taught to believe, this one may in truth 'change the world'."

Similarly, *The New York Times* had some reservations but also found "wisdom and stimulation" in the book. "Anyone who follows the regimen outlined here will, in a number of ways, help himself and his society," its critic commented.

Most reviewers for Catholic publications were full of praise, although a few criticized the book for its "modern cliches" and "pious slogans" — and for its insistence that one person, even one who was motivated, could have a serious impact on the secular world. The author gently deflected the criticism and plunged ahead with all he had to do for The Christophers. As a popular song of the day advised, it was time to "accentuate the positive" — and that's what Keller was determined to do.

One writer who would later analyze *You Can Change the World* and its impact was Richard Armstrong, Father Keller's successor as director of The Christophers. In his biography of the priest, *Out to Change the World* (1984), Armstrong provides some of Keller's own thoughts about the book (and his implicit acknowledgment of his critics), as expressed in a letter to his religious superior: "We have been purposely repetitious. The book is not intended to be read in one sitting — as a novel — but used as a reference or guidebook, with sections of it adapted to specific groups." In another section of the same letter, Father Keller thinly disguises his sense of pride in what he had accomplished. "We don't expect our book will be any world-beater," he wrote. "We are conscious of many imperfections in it. One thing in its favor, however — as far as we can check — there isn't anything else like it on the market, or we would have copied part of it! We have had to start off from scratch."

Armstrong described the book as "both a tribute to the power of Communism and an appeal to believers in God to become as active as the Communists in promoting their own beliefs.... Repeatedly, he [Father Keller] insisted on beating the Communists at their own game by running for office, learning parliamentary procedure, and staying at meetings till the bitter end."

If the American people of the late 1940s were apprehensive about the coming years, they also remained idealists. It was that idealism that Keller tapped into so effectively, reminding his readers that they were the ones who could determine their *own* future. It was all up to them, a point he made clear early in *You Can Change the World*. He advised them to seek careers in areas where they could affect others: communications, government service, labor-management relations, education. Christophers were not just being asked to do something positive, he wrote; they would be involved in nothing less than a battle for a better world.

A tall order, that, but it caught hold. In the process it catapulted The Christophers into a national presence, and made Keller himself into something of a celebrity. The book was nothing less than a sensation. Readers wrote in by the hundreds and eventually by the thousands to tell him how *You Can Change the World* had indeed changed their own lives.

A Long Island housewife said the book had altered her way of thinking. "You are the first person," she wrote to Father Keller, "who has filled me with the desire to *live* my religion." Another woman said the book inspired her to enroll in law school, and at the time the letter was written she was maintaining a B+ average, well on her way to her degree. As Armstrong put it, the book gave hope to thousands of people who might otherwise have sat back and done nothing. All they needed was a salesman like James Keller to stir them into action.

No one will ever know, of course, how many people *You Can Change the World* actually reached, or how deep an impact it had on the course of world events. But one story, related in Armstrong's biography, offers a tantalizing sense of possibility in that direction.

In the early 1960s Richard Nixon, then out of office and working for a New York law firm, was speaking informally at a dinner party being held in his honor. Keller happened to be one of the guests on hand, and heard the future president say that on the day in 1949 when he first took his seat in Congress as a California Republican another freshman representative gave him a book. "You might enjoy this," the other new man said.

The book was *You Can Change the World*. And the other freshman congressman was a Democrat from Massachusetts named John F. Kennedy.

The Issues

For some living in postwar America, Communism was just a system of government. True, it dominated to an overwhelming degree the lives of those who lived under it. But the problem, if indeed there was a problem, was a distant one — those people were halfway around the world.

For Father James Keller, though, Communism was much more than that. It was cruel, immoral and unjust, to be sure. But beyond that it was a menace, a threat to the American way of life, very real and very close at hand. Communists and their allies were already at work in our society, stealthily advancing toward positions of influence in key occupational areas, ready to impose their godless will on an unsuspecting nation.

The Maryknoll priest was hardly alone. Many shared his concerns. Some tackled the situation stridently; others exploited it for their own ends. Neither of those approaches had anything to do with Keller's style. He was sure that if enough Americans knew about the danger and if they took the proper and positive steps to overcome it — if, indeed, they became "Christophers" — the peril of Communism could be contained. He put those thoughts in a book, and what happened after that was truly historic. *You Can Change the World* might not have changed the entire world. But beyond question, it changed many, many lives.

As noted earlier, Father Keller's book came along at the right time. By 1948 the thrill of the Allied victory in World War II, which had ended three years earlier, was already giving way to concerns about the future. For many those concerns were genuine, but somewhat unfocused. Keller was determined to put a face on them, and to address them with startling clarity. They all seemed to begin and end with Communism.

"Make no mistake about it," he wrote. "We are at the crossroads of civilization. We stand on the brink of the greatest peace the world has ever enjoyed — or the most terrible nightmare of misery and chaos that mankind has ever known.

"The issue is clear and narrows down to what is truth with regard to the human being. If he is not a creature of God and the noblest act of God, with rights from Him, then he is just a clod of earth or the merest tool of the almighty State. He must be one or the other. He cannot be both."

Keller peppered the original text of *You Can Change the World* with stories of Communists infiltrating their way into the mainstream of American society — in schools, in labor unions, in the press and the world of entertainment, even in the government.

"Ever on the job, they use every possible medium to further

their purpose," he wrote. "They are in a race for man's soul."

Communists owed whatever success they achieved to their ability to deceive Americans about their true purpose until it was too late, Keller said. That's why it was so important to recognize them early on and to overcome their evil with the goodness that belongs naturally to Americans of faith. That, he added, takes work, and the work is of overriding importance:

> One of the best ways to cure a starving patient is to build him up with good, nourishing food. The best way to cure this disease in our society is to build up society itself with good ideas and ideals and to eliminate those which are evil.
>
> Our responsibility to our fellowmen in this respect is tremendous. Christ has put in our hands the Divine medicinal power, the restorative power of love. Ours is the mission to bring that love to all mankind, to "go to all men" and "to all nations." There is no substitute, no short cut.

All of which led, of course, to The Christophers — where the emphasis has always been on the positive. Father Keller was not confrontational by nature, shunning the chip-on-the-shoulder style in favor of a calm appeal to faith, reason and love of country. Too, he had a firm confidence in the value system of the average person. If he was writing for the masses, as indeed he was, he was an author who knew his audience.

The value system he had in mind placed a strong emphasis on patriotism, optimism and a sense of fairness, all of which were rooted in faith. To underscore the latter point, he approvingly quoted from Clare Booth Luce, the author and one-time member of Congress (and notable convert to Catholicism): "If the day ever comes when the men and women of our Western Civilization desert completely the historic concept of man as a child of God with free will and an immortal soul — if the day comes, in short, when we, too, go over to 'scientific materialism' — on that day not all our oil or gold in the ground, nor our assembly lines, nor our air forces, nor our navies ... shall save us. On that day freedom will perish in the totalitarian night of the world."

Truth and freedom go together, Keller repeatedly reminded readers of *You Can Change the World*. One thing that terrifies the godless of the world, he wrote, is "the fear that some day all those who believe in Christ will wake up and start acting their beliefs." When that happens, he continued, "most of the great problems which plague mankind will disappear overnight."

What problems would James Keller be writing about today? Nearly six decades after his ground-breaking book first appeared, what issues would he want modern-day Christophers to tackle?

We have already seen that even in the latter stages of his career, Keller was still doing all that he could to change the world. And so to begin with, it's safe to assume that he would still be leading people onward, actively urging them to take charge of their destiny by living their faith.

One thing that might surprise him is the near disappearance of global Communism as a threat to the democratic way of life. In *You Can Change the World* he emphatically downplayed that possibility. At the same time, however, he wrote that even if world-wide Communism *should* vanish, the conditions that make possible *all* forms of totalitarianism would still remain. How right he was. For example:

On the international level, we are consumed by the constant threat of terrorism — a danger that Keller could scarcely have imagined, and one that threatens to paralyze our entire future.

Here at home the threat of secularism that loomed so large in 1948 is larger still — infinitely so — as a new century gets under way. Standards of behavior — in the trappings of modern culture, and in life in general — have all but collapsed. Society lacks a moral compass; "anything goes" is less a slogan than it is a way of life.

These perils and others would concern Father Keller, of course, but his counsel would still be to follow the same positive steps he wrote about sixty years ago. He would most likely find a receptive audience, too, because even in the midst of today's turmoil men and women sense a quiet yearning, even a deep need, for direction in their lives.

Consider these thoughts from Michael Goodwin, a columnist in the *New York Daily News,* who wrote this shortly after the death of Pope John Paul II in April of 2005. He wrote specifically of the papacy, and its place in the lives of everyone in the world. But his words carried an even more fundamental message.

"The papacy matters to us non-Catholics because we live in a world gone mad for the latest fad," he wrote. "Most of us are moral transients, our technology-fueled culture crashing at warp speed through one taboo after another. Old-fashioned virtue is hailed only if it makes you feel good.

"Many elements of the modern world — media, movies, fashion, the arts — conspire to trash tradition and work against families with children. Actors, athletes, even porn stars are the new arbiters of right and wrong. Wealth has become synonymous with wisdom, fame with worth.

"Ultimately, it's all unsatisfying, this orgy of glitz and glitter and greed. Most of us know that, of course, but we still spend too much time and energy trying to win the race, to get more. And if we don't get what we want, we hire a lawyer to get it for us. Or we steal it.

"Merely by existing, the Pope reminds us of our foolishness. A sighting of him on TV, a casual reference, can summon the soul to embrace timeless truths, however fleetingly.

"A strong Pope does that and much, much more. A strong Pope, such as John Paul II, reminds us not only of the kingdom of heaven, but leads us to better lives now."

"Timeless truths"

Those are the truths that Father Keller expressed, all those years ago. At the time they were directed specifically against the inroads of global Communism. A different set of challenges faces the world in our own time. But the answers that Keller offered back in 1948 are the answers to today's problems as well. That, in fact, might have been James Keller's greatest gift: his ability to apply the fundamentals of faith and tradition in a way that lets us see their relevance to the dangers of any age. His formula, as he conceded, was a simple one. He prescribed honesty, courage, a willingness to get involved, a positive outlook, and a love of country and of those around us based on a deep and abiding faith.

They happened to be the building blocks of The Christophers. They also happen to be the building blocks of The Christophers today.

The Christophers

In the summer of 2005 an envelope addressed to The Christophers contained an extraordinary and heartwarming surprise. It was an account of a life of service to others lived by a Michigan man, which he wrote shortly before his death a few months earlier. Along with it was a cover letter from the man's daughter, pointing out that it was The Christophers who sparked her father's remarkable career.

Remarkable is hardly the word. The man, a veteran of World War II, heard about the Christopher movement, liked its teaching that "It's better to light one candle than to curse the darkness," signed up for the Christopher Leadership Course — and never looked back. He began with an active role in the labor movement, helping to ward off a Communist-inspired takeover in his union local. He helped the poor through the Catholic Worker movement, took a prominent role in the Christian Family Movement, and coordinated religious education activities in his parish.

The man was just getting warmed up. He took pioneering roles in interracial adoption, Marriage Encounter and Engaged Encounter, Cursillo, conducted food and clothing drives, helped restore calm in the face of a deadly riot, established the first community home for mentally handicapped children in his state, founded neighborhood homes for the unwanted and the needy, opened his own home to foster children, and to adults who simply needed a place to stay.

There was all this and more, always with the encouragement of his wife and family. And looking back on it, he reflected, simply: "As usual, if you are doing the Lord's work and His will you will never tire, for the joy of Jesus is active!"

His daughter's note to The Christophers carried a note of understandable pride.

"My Dad made a difference in many, many lives," she wrote. "He always credited our Heavenly Father first, for the gifts that were bestowed on him, and then to you, The Christophers, who helped him focus on God's light and how to use the talents he was blessed with. The Christophers were the cornerstone of my Dad's life."

The story was exceptional, to be sure, and The Christophers are grateful for it. But mail of this nature comes into The Christophers' office every day — with thanks for favors, acknowledgments of lives turned around, wonder at the power of prayer. A prisoner might write with gratitude for an upbeat News Note that came at just the right time. A young mother will express thanks for the inspiration she finds each day on the Christopher Web site. A positive television message on "Christopher Closeup" leads a man to write: "Thank you for being there for me in my rebirth into the wonders of my faith."

Then there was the Massachusetts man who wrote to say this: "I truly believe that the Christopher message has had more impact on my life than all the other education I have received. The Christophers taught me that I could make a difference — that I did not have to be the most brilliant or the most successful. I hope when I stand before our God one day, He will say, 'You tried to light the way — you tried to be a Christopher'."

These responses and thousands more like them stand as reminders that The Christophers and their message are alive and well, sixty years after Father Keller launched the movement. A new generation continues to build on his work, as dedicated as ever to convincing people that they can make a difference, that they can change the world.

Father Keller was thrilled — and perhaps a little surprised as well — with the way The Christophers grew and matured. According to Richard Armstrong, Keller thought at the outset that The Christophers would last for only a few years and then die out. But as time went on, and it became evident that the movement would be around for a while, he saw to it that The Christophers had a proper home, and also began thinking about a successor.

The headquarters, a seven-story building at 12 East 48th Street in Manhattan, was a gift (made in 1966) from John and Barbara Newington, with whom Keller spent many weekends at their home in Greenwich, Connecticut. The man he groomed as his successor was Armstrong, later his biographer, at the time a Maryknoll priest and a skilled writer who got along well with Keller. He held the position from 1969, when Keller retired, to 1977. Though no longer a priest or a member of Maryknoll, he retained a close connection to The Christophers until his death in 2001.

Keller's best-known successor as director of The Christophers was Father John Catoir, a priest of the Diocese of Paterson, New Jersey who followed Armstrong and stayed on until 1995. A gifted speaker and prolific author whose personality helped to acquaint a younger generation with The Christophers, Catoir also gave the organization a new level of prominence within

Catholic communication circles. He was succeeded by Msgr. Thomas McSweeney and Msgr. James Lisante, both of whom served for limited periods before being recalled for service in their home dioceses.

As the new century began The Christophers' Board of Directors hoped to locate another priest-director, but eventually realized that the pool of qualified and available priests was not nearly as large as it once was. Ultimately, in 2003 the Board chose Dennis Heaney, a veteran of the Catholic press and a talented communicator himself, as the first lay person to head The Christophers. With the title of President, his leadership has been marked by a period of growth and a re-commitment to fundamental Christopher principles.

There is more than a touch of irony in the fact that as the years went on, Father Keller fretted that he might be holding The Christophers back by his own "limited vision." It's ironic because the more the present-day Christopher organization patterns itself on the Keller original, the more successful it seems to be.

Virtually all contemporary Christopher activities, for example, follow to one degree or another those that date back to Keller's time — News Notes, *Three Minutes a Day,* Christopher Closeup, the Christopher Leadership Course, the Christopher Awards and more. (An obvious exception is the Christopher Web site, since the Internet was an unknown quantity when Father Keller was alive.) An arresting photograph of the founder now commands a place of honor in the lobby of the 48th Street building, and his portrait in oils was rescued from storage and placed near the entrance to the President's office. Keller's photo now graces all Christopher fund-raising material — and since it has been restored there, the appeals have shown a healthy and steady upward climb.

Father Keller's presence, in short, colors everything The Christophers do today.

Delivering the homily at a Mass in 2000 marking the 100th

anniversary of Father Keller's birth, New York Auxiliary Bishop William J. McCormack, then national director of the Society for the Propagation of the Faith, noted the many ways in which the priest's work had foreshadowed the developments of Vatican Council II, calling him "a true prophet for our times."

"We know that it is better to light one candle than to lament the darkness," Bishop McCormack said. "We know it is, indeed, infinitely better, because the candle we light is Jesus Christ, the true Light of the world, a light that burned forth so brightly from within the person and life of James Keller."

Both with simplicity and with profound truth, that sums up the man whose life continues to inspire The Christophers. That inspiration is reflected, too, in the Christopher mission statement:

"The mission of The Christophers is to encourage people of all ages, and from all walks of life, to use their God-given talents to make a positive difference in the world. The mission is best expressed in The Christophers' motto: 'It's better to light one candle than to curse the darkness.'

"We believe that each person has a God-given mission to fulfill, a particular job to do that has been given to no one else. Love and truth come to us through God, but these gifts are not ours to keep. By sharing them with others each of us becomes a Christ-bearer, a 'Christopher' in the most fundamental sense of that word.

"It is through our literature, broadcasts, awards and leadership courses that we at The Christophers work toward our mission, bringing positive and constructive values into the mainstream of life. To encourage personal responsibility we have no meetings, no memberships and no dues. All are welcome to join us, knowing that in embracing the Christopher mission they will share one overriding commitment: the love of all people for the love of God."

In The Christophers, and in the lives of untold thousands of people, Father Keller's work goes forward. Here, just as he wrote them, are the words that started it all.

Prologue

One hot, dust-laden day in Samaria long ago, a woman came to the Well of Jacob, just off the high road from Jerusalem to Galilee, to draw water ... unaware that she was that day to become one of the outstanding instruments in a new program which was to revolutionize the world.

It was about noon, and the place was deserted but for the solitary figure of a Man. He was obviously a traveler and, to a Samaritan woman, just as obviously a Jew, and He sat with His back resting wearily against the stone parapet of the well. The chattering women of the village and their noisy offspring had long since returned to their homes, but the woman, head high and face proud, made no move to speak to the stranger. She was an outcast even among her own people, because she had taken to herself five husbands. Yet in her eyes, which had seen much and had not liked what they saw, was a hunger for something even she would have been at a loss to explain.

Leaning forward, she hooked the water pot to the rope coiled about the top of the well and turned the windlass, unmindful of the Man watching her. As the vessel, brimming over, was pulled to the surface, the Man spoke: "*Give Me a drink,*" He said, and in her surprise that a stranger, and a Jew, at that, should speak to her, she offered Him a measure of water. When He had drunk and the woman's puzzled "*How is it that you, a Jew ask a drink of me who am a woman of Samaria?*" (John 4:9) had been answered with a reply that gave a clue to His identity, the Man bade her, *"Go call your husband and come back."*

Taken off guard by this strange and sudden command, the woman yet sensed quite well in His quiet dignity the superiority and authority of the Speaker. Tears squeezing through the corners of her eyes, with an instinct for self-preservation that counseled against revealing all the sordidness of her life, she answered, *"I have no husband."*

There was a pause before the Man made reply. He looked at her with an eye of complete and kindly understanding. He knew she had intended to deceive Him but, without rebuke, He finished her admission for her by saying, *"You are right in saying 'I have no husband'; for you have had five husbands, and the one you have now is not your husband."*

A sudden fear widened the woman's eyes, but in a moment was gone. Left only was the strange hunger to which she gave voice in a question that was also meant to distract Him. His answer was to tell her more, but this time of Himself and of His work. In later years when He was gone, she was to recall the day she had met Him and humbly thank God that in those early years she had heard from His own lips the declaration of His identity.

Now, however, joy in her new knowledge could not be contained. She felt she had actually been commissioned — individually and personally — to go and share that knowledge with as many others as she could. She did not waste a moment. Leaving her water pot in her haste, she hurried to the village. Behind her she left the Man Who, by this time, had been rejoined by His followers. The surprise on their faces at finding their Master talking with her she ignored, just as she failed to be mindful of the same old sneers and loathing which greeted her in the village. With beating heart, to all whom she saw she proclaimed triumphantly, *"Come and see a Man Who has told me everything I have ever done. Could this be the Messiah?"*

"Thus," as Archbishop Alban Goodier puts it so well, "was that poor woman, that poor, sinful, heretical, Samaritan woman, chosen to be the *first apostle of Christ Jesus in this world.*"

Drawn out of herself, her words carried the ring of conviction to her listeners and, as the Gospel narrative continues: *"They therefore left the city and were on their way to Him.... When the Samaritans came to him, they asked him to stay with them."* And Jesus, accepting their invitation, *"stayed there two days."*

After He had departed, the villagers discussed among themselves all that He had said to them. Finally, coming to the woman, they told her somewhat ungraciously, *"It is no longer because of what you said that we believe, for we have heard for ourselves, and we know that this is truly the Savior of the world."*

But the woman knew, and we know through the utter simplicity of the Gospel account how an outcast, a violator of the laws of human decency, was chosen as the connecting link, the "silken cord," between Christ and those who might never have known Him, but for her. To all appearances, she was the most unlikely messenger of Christ imaginable. She was also the first to go through the bitter experience for which every Christopher must be prepared — discovering that those she had brought to Christ, far from being grateful, were inclined to resent the part played by her and determined to minimize it. Yet, in the newness of her life, it probably mattered little to her that she had once more decreased in the estimation of her neighbors. The important thing to her was that Christ had increased.

In truth, did she "go," even hurry, into the marketplace as a Christ-bearer. And, in going, she is an example for all to imitate who would bear Christ to others.

In these disturbing times there is a thrilling challenge in the realization that the world itself can be better because we are in it. No matter what our circumstances or failings, we can yet do *more* than say, *"Your will be done on earth."* We can, with Christ's help, actually make this tired old world of ours *the prelude to heaven!* And since that is what God wants it to be, truly it is a great time to be alive. Now — and for all eternity — we can look with deep consolation on the part we have played, no matter how small or insignificant, in shaping for the better the destiny of all mankind!

YOU CAN CHANGE THE WORLD

"Everything's All Right in Kokomo!"

A few months ago while traveling through Indiana, giving talks in the smaller towns and cities of the state, one thing more than any other impressed itself on me. It was the *quality* of the people who made up the various audiences — farmers and factory workers, small businessmen and housewives — in short, the sound, solid folk who are the backbone of America.

No wild-eyed, irrational, heads-in-the-clouds visionaries were they. On the contrary, on their faces were the calm, down-to-earth expressions of people possessed of an honest sense of values. In their eyes was the quiet confidence born of such knowledge.

If ever a description fitted a group of individuals, it was the phrase, "salt of the earth." And in one talk frankly I told them so.

"If we had people with your plain common sense teaching in our colleges, running our government, our trade unions, writing our newspapers, magazines, books, radio programs and movie scenarios," I said, "everything would be pretty much all right with our country... and the world."

After the talk one middle-aged gentleman came up to me. He seemed neither angry nor pleased with what I had just observed but, taking my hand, said simply, "I come from Kokomo ... and everything's all right in Kokomo!"

If he had launched into a tirade of criticism or disagreement, his words would not have startled me half as much as that quiet statement of fact: "I come from Kokomo... and everything's all right in Kokomo."

Though he failed to realize it, that one little remark sums up only too well what probably is the chief obstacle to peace in the world. Most *good* people are taking care only of themselves while most *evil* people are taking care of everyone else. Most people with good ideas are thinking in small circles, in terms of a thousand separate "Kokomos" while the people who are out to wreck our civilization are planning and acting on a long-term, daring scale — in terms of centuries and over the span of the world!

The Hope That Is "Kokomo"

To know that everything is all right in Kokomo, however, is encouraging... thank God for it. But for us, the refreshing hope in that knowledge is to release into the bloodstream of the whole country and the arteries of the world the confined goodness which makes Kokomo and communities like it what they are.

And tens upon tens of thousands of people of every age and in all walks of life are doing just that right now! They are getting out of themselves and into the thick of things. They are exerting their tremendous influence for good and hastening the day when peace will once more come to all mankind.

And that word "tremendous" is not misused.

For instance, still fresh in people's memories is the recent gigantic letter-writing campaign directed by the American people to the people of Italy, telling them what freedom and democracy mean in the United States and what they would mean to Italians if they only appreciated these rights enough to work for them.

Not just hundreds, or even thousands, but literally millions of letters went out from people of Italian descent in every section of this nation to their relatives in the "old country." Yet that campaign didn't start by itself — somebody started it. And that somebody was *one man*, a barber in Southampton, Long Island, N.Y.

He had left Italy himself in 1913 and had come to the United States, determined to become a living part of our democracy for the rest of his days. He'd married, raised a family, and found life good. As the years went by, however, two things began to bother him. One was the constant stream of criticism from many quarters about what was wrong with our government and with the world in general. The second thing — and which irritated him even more than the first — was that those who did the complaining never seemed to do anything about making conditions any better.

Following World War II when news of millions of Italians flirting with Communism reached the American press, his patience reached the breaking point. He decided to do something about it personally.

First he wrote to his own relatives in St. Catherine, Sicily. Next he wrote to his wife's relatives who lived near the same town, telling all of them what the free way of life meant in America. Then he got his oldest boy, a doctor, and his oldest girl, a dietician, to write. He sent letters to the President and to all the newspapers in the New York area, asking for their support. The reaction to the idea was invariably good — but invariably it was accompanied with regrets that the project was too big to handle. Various organizations which he approached personally received him with smiles and wished him well… and that was all.

Faced with having the whole idea collapse on the spot, this barber still wouldn't quit. He kept writing and contacting his friends who had relatives in the old country, asking them to lend a hand. Gradually — providentially — the idea began to catch fire. Businessmen, young GI brides, housewives, veterans groups, civic societies, and religious leaders took up the fight. Soon a steady trickle (that in no time at all became a torrent) of heartfelt letters of thanks started coming back from Italy, promising to push the democratic concept of life. The result: hundreds of thousands of people in America began to do something no other agency or official group could possibly have done — reach the hearts of the Italian people.

And remember, one man started it all. One man, personally, was responsible for all of this because he got out of his own little world with its little ideas and into the big world with all its breathtaking potentialities.

Other Situations — Other Workers

Other men and other women in less spectacular ways, perhaps, but with equally far-reaching results, are carrying their individual Kokomos into the battle for a better world.

In the University of Wisconsin at this moment one particular teacher is there at a great personal sacrifice simply because he finally realized how much more good he could do in the classroom than by pursuing a successful business career. Once he had been a teacher but had given it up, as he put it, to "make more money on the outside." The money had come, all right, but with it no real peace of mind.

The situation annoyed him. More than that, it puzzled him. Here he was with almost everything anyone could want and he wasn't happy. It was fantastic, unbelievable, yet until he happened across a Christopher pamphlet he was at a loss to know the reason. Reading it, he found out. In getting ahead in the world, in thinking only of himself, he was neglecting the good of others, particularly the youngsters he had been trained to teach. So — back to the classroom he went … and back to the satisfaction of knowing he was doing the most for his fellow men in the best way he knew how.

In a sense this teacher-turned-businessman-turned-teacher had unconsciously been conducting an experiment with himself. He had been testing his own reactions to a problem which involved engrossing himself in selfish rather than selfless interests. And he had found the formula unsatisfactory. Only when the proper equation or relationship between himself and his neighbor was realized, did he count the experiment a success.

And speaking of experiments, just recently a scientist in the research laboratory of the Eastman Kodak Company, who had learned about the Christophers and what they were doing, sent us this letter:

"You're on the right track," he wrote. "I've been in the scientific field most of my life and have seen the wonderful things it's done. Lately, however, I've noticed a pagan trend becoming more apparent. Much of our scientific development in this country proceeds from the old German school which threw out the idea of God and the supernatural, and paved the way for Hitler. The only way to correct this condition, as you say, is to bring back Christian values into the teaching end of science. Maybe I can help in this. Anyway, I'm giving up my present job and becoming a science teacher, even though the salary will be considerably less."

At a convention on the West Coast recently, the world's need for democracy was being discussed by the delegates at considerable length and with varying shades of opinion. In a corner of the huge meeting hall a housewife sat listening intently as the talk flowed on for the better part of two hours. Though she kept her silence, inside her was an undercurrent of excitement that was in sharp contrast to her earlier decision to pass up the convention and let her alternate go in her place. She'd felt, well ... so inadequate. Conventions were something new to her. She knew nothing about their methods of procedure nor even what each delegate was supposed to do, and she almost made up her mind that it was useless for her to attend. Then the thought occurred to her that if everyone passed up the opportunity to do something constructive for the country — even if that something was very small — the nation could be lost by default.

Quietly, she listened to what the other delegates had to say, the feeling of excitement inside her now mingled with a mounting impatience at their ideas on democracy which sounded so confused and superficial. Finally, she stood up and quietly suggested to the convention chairman that it might be well to define democracy. "What does the word mean?" she asked, and listened to the murmur of surprise that swept the hall.

Several delegates offered halting, uncertain replies. When they'd finished, the housewife stood up again. "It's interesting to note," she observed, "that many definitions have been submitted, yet not one has included the basic idea which our Founding Fathers considered so important that they put it right at the beginning of the Declaration of Independence, namely: each individual man, woman and child receives his rights from God, not from the State, and one of the chief purposes of the State is to protect and respect those God-given rights."

When she sat down, no one was more surprised than she at the volley of applause that greeted her words. In one simple statement she had distinguished between Christian democracy and pagan totalitarianism.

What this woman did personally and individually typifies the whole spirit of the Christopher approach. As one man (himself interested in the field of labor relations) put it in a recent letter from San Francisco:

"The magic of the Christopher idea — the shift from selfish defensive to unselfish offensive — has made me happier than I have been in a long time and in such a fundamental way.... Now I shall plunge into the study of labor legislation with added fire."

Here, There and Everywhere

In New York a few months ago a stockbroker whose business gave him ample opportunity to feel the pulse of the nation became alarmed when he realized that many who had made amazing inroads in this country, especially in the field of government, did not have our best interests at heart. His business associates, apparently, did not realize the danger, but since he did, it was up to him to do something about it. His position in Wall Street involved high-level administrative skills, so he decided to try for a job in the State Department in Washington … until he realized there were his wife and children to be considered. They had always been used to the best of everything, the finest clothes, the most modern luxuries in the home, and his wife in particular prized such possessions quite highly. If he went to Washington, he'd get far less money that he was making in New York.

Weeks of talking things over followed until, at last, they made their decision. Sacrifice or not, they'd make the change.

They've never regretted it. The ex-broker isn't "big time" any more — just a man in a government office doing a job. But what a job! His wife doesn't dress so well now, yet she doesn't care. There is a radiance on her face that was never there when she was considered very much the fashion-plate of style-conscious Manhattan. *Doing things for love of one's fellow man does that to people.*

A Baptist lawyer down in Texas is another who is finding that out, too. A man of about forty-five, he had been a captain in Army Intelligence during the recent war. And what he saw of the attempts of godless people to undermine our country made him fighting mad — not at anyone in particular — just fighting mad to do something about it.

Somehow he heard about the Christophers and, not long ago when I passed through Texas, he made it his business to see me. He asked my advice; but, before I gave it, I put just two questions to him:

"Do you believe in the basic idea that our Founding Fathers put in the Declaration of Independence — that man is a child of God and gets his rights from God? — that the problem of the State is to protect those rights?"

"I sure do," he answered.

"Are you willing to do something really constructive about it?"

"I sure am," came back the emphatic reply. "I'll even give up half my law practice to do it. That's how important I think it is!"

My suggestion to him was simply to go around and give as many talks as he could — at business functions, civic meetings, social gatherings, wherever the opportunity presented itself, and to encourage people with good ideas to get into the four great fields of education, labor management, government, and the writing end of newspapers, radio, motion pictures, television and so on.

I told him, also, to try and have each person who heard him to get at least one other person to do the same thing, to get them working *as hard* putting basic American ideals *into* these fields as the doers of evil work trying to pull them *out*.

"Better to Light One Candle Than to Curse the Darkness"

If he succeeds in doing just that, and if the people who hear him follow suit, then the darkness of confusion, of evil, and of error in that part of the world, at least, will be illuminated by a light that cannot — and will not — be put out. Instead of complaining about *evil,* they will be doing *good.*

An old Chinese proverb points up that fact so simply, yet so dramatically. "Better to light one candle," it goes, "than to curse the darkness." For a young woman in a small California town, doing that meant the difference between a life of sickness and pain and grumbling frustration, and a life that has been — and still is — an inspiration to everyone around her.

Weakened by a series of recurring epileptic fits, her condition was aggravated to the point that hospitalization was the only course left open to her. Lying in bed, hour upon weary hour, gave her plenty of time to think about the future. She felt sorry for herself, but after a time even self-pity became a trifle tiresome.

Looking around for something different to occupy her time, she got an idea. Perhaps if she tried to forget about her own troubles and tried to help others ... no, that wasn't quite it. Perhaps if she tried to help others *first*, then her own troubles might seem less important, less hopeless.

Though "no literary genius," as she put it, she did have some flair for writing. So she asked the hospital authorities to contact the editor of the town newspaper. "I want to write a column," she told him. "A column that will try to make people concentrate on ... well, the good in life around them instead of always doing just the opposite." And she almost added, "like I've been doing."

The editor agreed to give her a chance. Within three or four weeks after the column first appeared, letters began pouring in, thanking her, giving her a pat on the back for what she was trying to do.

And from that very first day on, this same young woman has rarely suffered another attack of epilepsy!

Doctors familiar with the case have not tried to minimize the change in her. Instead, they point out that the "getting out of herself," and out of her own narrow world, has given her a purpose in life, has done away with the mental and emotional frustration which, in their opinion, was apparently responsible for a serious physical disorder. And, while not attempting to generalize, they add that they know of similar cases where the cure was within the person himself as much as in any medical treatment.

For Each Life — Purpose

To some of us, realization of this fact comes easily. But to others, it comes only after some tremendous experience has shaken them out of their complacency and self-satisfaction.

A young ex-naval officer had spent five-and-one-half years on active service during the recent war, both with the Board of Economic Warfare and with the Photographic Division of the Armed Forces. Both jobs called for technical skill and an extraordinary capacity to evaluate material and, because of the complexities of modern warfare, evaluate men as well.

However, when he was returned to inactive duty and began getting into the feel of civilian life, he found something had happened to him in the time he'd been away. While in uniform, he'd had a purpose — to help win for himself and his countrymen a victorious peace. All the inconvenience, the suffering, the ever-present threat of death had been made more bearable because of that.

Now that he was back in civilian clothes he wanted his life to have a purpose also, a worthwhile goal to work toward, some field where he could do some good for others as well as for himself. It didn't call for simply making money, either, as the offer of a well-paying job with a big New York banking house, while it tempted him, didn't persuade him to the point of acceptance.

The job meant security. But it also meant the plowing of an economic and social furrow that might become a rut as the years went by. So he decided, not without regret, "That's not for me."

Well, how about the movies? In Europe, serving with the Photographic Division, he'd worked with several prominent Hollywood technicians and directors. Perhaps there was a place for him out there. But again, a blank wall. Oh, he was offered jobs, all right — good ones, too. Yet they paralleled too closely the Wall Street offer: money, nothing more.

Discouraging? Most assuredly, yes! Yet, somehow the movies, their creative values, and their wonderful potential for the communication of good to millions of people, still stuck in his mind. Driving along in his car one night with a friend who happened to be a Christopher, he asked for and got a solution to his dilemma.

The answer, briefly, was this: as an exhibitor of motion pictures — that is, as an independent exhibitor — he would be in a position to encourage movies that were both entertaining and decent. And he could weed out and refuse to show any film that didn't meet these standards.

This ex-naval officer knew next to nothing about this phase of the film industry. But he decided to learn.

At a salary that was a pittance compared to his Wall Street offer, he got a job in order to learn the field from the ground up. By the end of eighteen months — remember, he had a purpose — he had learned his work so well that with the help of a bank loan he was able to buy his own theater in an upstate New York college town. And, incidentally, he's making more money than he would have earned if he'd taken the job first offered him in Wall Street. A motion picture executive, noting his progress, commented recently that such a theater might well be the start of a string of theaters across the country similarly dedicated to showing only *good* screen plays.

More important at the present, however, is the fact that this man has already influenced the lives of thousands of people by giving them the best in screen entertainment. "If a picture doesn't deserve to be shown, I'll not show it, even if there's nothing else to put on the screen in its place," he announced not long ago. "If that happens, I'll close down the theater for a couple of days and put out a sign explaining why."

In his spare time this Christopher has completed a law course begun before he entered service and has also concerned himself in many activities offering opportunities to serve the general good.

The Importance of One Little Light

What this one Christopher did should be an inspiration to everyone who would truly bear Christ. Once a million men and women like him carry their light into the darkness of confusion, misinformation and error, then this groping old earth of ours will truly come to reflect the brightness of Him Who is the Light of the world.

Those who witnessed a postwar ceremonial at the Los Angeles Coliseum just after V-J Day can appreciate the physical accuracy of that statement. More than 100,000 spectators had jammed the huge stadium to witness a mighty pageant in honor of the city's war heroes. Thanks to the magic of Hollywood, the arena had been transformed into a terrifyingly realistic battle scene. Exploding land mines shook the earth, batteries of army tanks roared across the stadium, a mass formation of B-29s swooped down over the watching throng. The noise was deafening and the effect thundering and overpowering, as if to emphasize the helplessness and insignificance of the human individual in the face of so much mechanical might.

Then something strange happened. Suddenly all the outburst stopped and stepping to the microphone the master of ceremonies began to speak to the listening thousands.

"Perhaps you sometimes say to yourself," he began, "'My job isn't that important because it's such a little job.' But you're wrong. The most obscure person can be very important. Anyone here who wants to exert a far-reaching power may do so. Let me show you what I mean."

Abruptly, the giant searchlights that bathed every corner of the Coliseum were turned off. From day-like brightness the great arena was unexpectedly plunged into total darkness. Then the speaker struck a match, and in the blackness the tiny flame could be seen by everyone.

"Now you can see the importance of one little light," he said. "But suppose we *all* strike a light!"

From all over the stadium came the sound of matches being struck until, faster than it takes to tell, nearly 100,000 pinpoints of light lit up the summer night.

Everyone gasped with surprise. Quickly and effectively, there had been demonstrated to them the power of each single individual.

Coming out of the Coliseum and making our way through the crowds in the parking lot, we found ourselves thinking about how comparatively easy it would be to bring peace to a heartsick world if only enough of the wonderful people in it would make a constant effort to spread the light of truth, and combat the darkness of error.

People all over the earth are beginning to realize more and more that there is a very intimate connection between truth and freedom. Sobered by the scourge of war, even those opposed to religion are more disposed to admit the inescapable conclusion of what Christ meant when He said: "The Truth shall make you free" (John 8:32). Once a sufficient number of people realize that falsehood is nothing more than the absence of truth, just as darkness is the absence of light, hate the absence of love, and disease the absence of health, then there is high hope that this old world of ours will one day come to know the blessing of a real, lasting peace.

Anyone can help in this task. You can. I can. And, naturally, the closer we are to Christ the better Christophers we will be. Yes, no one is so far away from Christ that he or she cannot share in some measure in this tremendous undertaking.

And startling as it may seem, anyone who learns even one of Christ's Truths — and tries to spread that truth in the life-stream of his land — is beginning to be a Christopher, whether or not he realizes it. The more he does for Christ, the closer he draws to Christ. With each truth-bearer he will have the satisfaction of knowing that he can be a bearer of "the True Light which enlightens everyone" (John 1:9) in this world. They can be partners with Him Who said: *"I am the Way, and the Truth, and the Life"* (John 14:6).

Every one of us can be a bearer of Christ — a Christopher.

CHAPTER TWO

The Problem Has a Cure

"Those people who are not governed by God
will be ruled by tyrants."   *William Penn*

Over two hundred and fifty years ago when the charter of the
Commonwealth of Pennsylvania was being written, the Quaker,
William Penn, sounded that very warning. Today those words
have for us a far greater, even a life-and-death, significance.

Make no mistake about it. We are at the crossroads of civilization. We stand on the brink of the greatest peace the world
has ever enjoyed — or the most terrible nightmare of misery and
chaos that mankind has ever known.

The issue is clear and narrows down to what is truth with
regard to the human being. If he is not a creature of God and the
noblest act of God, with rights from Him, then he is just a clod
of earth or the merest tool of the almighty State. He must be one
or the other. He cannot be both.

The Greatest Obstacle

It seems evident that we've been unable to cope with the
thousand-and-one problems all over the globe which the cessa-

tion of World War II has brought. And these problems have become magnified as the earth has shrunk in proportion to the advances of modern science with its jet-propelled planes, faster than the speed of sound, and its atom bomb, which can level all humanity to the common denominator of a lifeless, fetid pulp.

But great as these problems are, perhaps the most formidable problem of all which we have failed so far to solve is represented by the force of those who would eliminate God from the face of the earth.

The greatest obstacle to finding a solution to this problem, as well as to most of the others, is the *apathy* which comes from our lack of understanding that we followers of Christ have the salvation of the world in our hands. Far too many people are deluded into believing that we are living in a brave, new world where everything is different, and values — human values — are not what they used to be.

But let's not fool ourselves. *It is still the same old world.* Conditions have changed drastically; still we are fundamentally the same. The world will never be more than we are. If the world is in bad shape, it's because too many of *us* are in bad condition.

Many people are inclined to think that once Communism is on the wane all over the globe, mankind will settle back automatically to an era of peace. Most emphatically, that cannot be true. Even if Communism were to disappear overnight — which it most certainly will not — the situation which makes *all* forms of totalitarianism possible still remains. And not only does it remain, it grows steadily worse. Those who fall for the attractive deceptions of the materialists are not merely those, oddly enough, who are economically insecure. In far greater numbers they are those who have no spiritual moorings, no fixed beliefs in the Fatherhood of God and the dignity of man.

Of course most Americans are *against* Communism now, just as they were against Nazism and Fascism. But they don't know what they are *for*. They talk vaguely about the "free way of life" and the need for democracy, yet most of them have only a faint idea of the Cause which makes these *effects* possible. They are unaware that every time this Cause is removed, out the window go the effects as well.

If this steady trend toward paganism continues, it is only a matter of time before our nation will collapse — more from deterioration from *within* than from any force *without*.

It Is Not Too Late to Save America

How to correct that problem? Actually, the answer is very simple. Just as one of the best ways to cure a starving patient is to build him up with good, nourishing food, the best way to cure this disease in our society is to build up society itself — with good ideas and ideals, and to eliminate those which are evil.

Our responsibility to our fellowmen in this respect is tremendous. Christ has put in our hands the Divine medicinal power, the restorative power of love. Ours is the mission to bring that love to all people, to "go to all men" and "to all nations." There is no substitute, no shortcut.

Those who have a burning love of God and of all people, not merely of self, will go to the greatest lengths to put a sense of brotherhood into practice. They will suffer everything to share that love with all humanity.

It is the Christopher thesis, therefore, that for the few among us who are bent on destruction, it should not be too difficult to find an equal number who will strive with even greater imagination and enterprise to show a devoted and continuing solicitude for all our brothers and sisters who are reached by no faith. As Christophers, as Christ-bearers, they will go into their very midst, into all the spheres that influence the destinies of mankind.

Most Americans, including that great number who are not members of organized worshiping communities, are blessed with an abundance of common sense. They are extremely fair when they *know* the facts and are seriously interested in getting fair play for all people of all nations. They most certainly are *not* atheistic. A Gallup poll revealed that ninety-four percent of Americans believe in God, three percent list themselves as "not knowing," and only another three percent put themselves down as atheists. Their present drift from religion is probably much less their fault than it is that of the followers of Christ who fail to "go" and "keep going" to them with the same determination and thoroughness displayed by Christ's enemies.

This is a far from normal state of affairs. The strength of American life is rooted in Christian truth, as an editorial in *Fortune* magazine recently pointed out:

"The basic teachings of Christianity are in its bloodstream," it said. *"The central doctrine of its political system — the inviolability of the individual — is a doctrine inherited from nineteen hundred years of Christian insistence upon the immortality of the soul."*

The first Americans acknowledged this. They believed in the supernatural, as every important document of colonial history shows. From Georgia to the Massachusetts Bay Colony they had respect and reverence for certain fundamental Christian principles which modern totalitarians and materialists seek to destroy. Among these truths are the following:

1. The existence of a personal God, Who has spoken to the world.
2. Jesus Christ, true God and true man.
3. The Ten Commandments.
4. The sacred character of the individual.
5. The sanctity of the lifelong marriage bond.
6. The sanctity of the home as the basic unit of the whole human family.

Father James Keller, MM

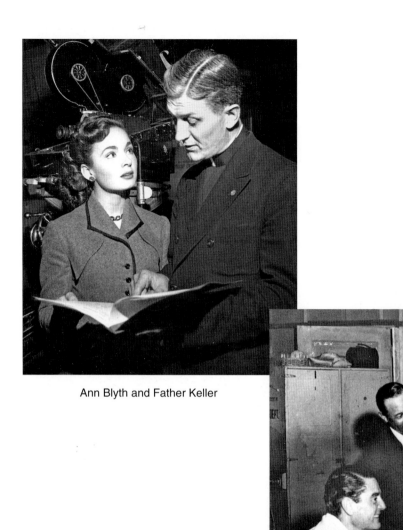

Ann Blyth and Father Keller

Shown in this photo with Father James Keller, Director of The Christophers, are some members of the cast of the successful 1951 film "You Can Change the World," including (left to right) Director Leo McCarey, Eddie "Rochester" Anderson, Ann Blyth, Jack Benny, Father Keller, Irene Dunne, Loretta Young, William Holden and Paul Douglas. Also appearing in the movie were Bing Crosby and Bob Hope.

Father Keller with
Jack Benny and
Eddie "Rochester"
Anderson

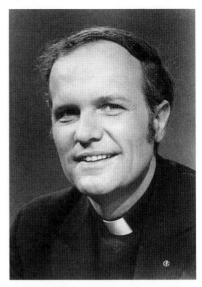

The late Richard Armstrong, above right, then a Maryknoll priest, was Father Keller's first successor as Director of The Christophers. He was followed by Father John Catoir, left, Director from 1978 to 1995.

Dennis Heaney, right, is President of The Christophers and is the first lay person to head the organization on a permanent basis. He is shown following a "Christopher Closeup" interview with Charles Osgood, the CBS radio and television broadcaster, who says *You Can Change the World* had a strong influence on his life.

7. The human rights of every person as coming from God, not from the State.
8. The right, based on human nature, to possess private property, with its consequent obligation to society.
9. Due respect for domestic, civil and religious authority.
10. Judgment after death.

These basic truths are only a portion of "all things" which Christ commissioned His Church to teach "all nations" (Matthew 28:19-20). Upon them, the early Americans wisely built our nation. Proof that recognition of them was much more than lip-service to eternal truths, that they were actually a part of the lives of the men and women who first settled our country, is found in one account after another of the early days of this country's history.

For example, in the field of education alone, 140 years before the signing of the Declaration of Independence the motto of Harvard University was given as *In Christi Gloriam* (For the Glory of Christ). The university's founder, John Harvard, was referred to as a *"godly gentleman and a man of learning"* in the legislative act in 1638 that authorized the founding of this world-famed institution. And, during the administration of the school's first president, Master Dunster, one of the student directives was even more explicit in emphasizing the spiritual values that characterized all phases of early American life. *"Let every student be plainly instructed,"* the directive reads, *"and earnestly pressed to consider well, the main end of his life and studies is to know God and Jesus Christ which is eternal life.... Christ [is] the only foundation of all sound knowledge and learning."*

"We Hold These Truths to Be Self-Evident"

Thus these early Americans set the pace in acknowledging the Fatherhood of God and the Brotherhood of man, and what was good enough for them should at least represent the minimum good for us. At any rate, their beliefs were good enough for our Founding Fathers who, right in the beginning, wrote these words into the Declaration of Independence: *"We hold these truths to be self-evident, that all men are created equal, that they are endowed by their Creator with certain inalienable Rights, that among these are Life, Liberty, and the pursuit of Happiness."*

And again quoting from the same document:

"To secure these rights governments are instituted among men, deriving their just powers from the consent of the governed."

The Founding Fathers, you see, were most explicit. They were God-fearing men. For them the idea of God had to be integrated with everything if men and women were not to forget that their rights, liberties, and life itself come from their Creator. They must have feared that, in the years ahead, those who would destroy America might subtly deny this *Truth*. So, leaving nothing to chance, they were most positive.

They took pains to emphasize the fact that the natural law itself depends on God, when they wrote: "When in the course of human events, it becomes necessary for one people to dissolve the political bands, which have connected them with another, and to assume among the powers of the earth, the separate and equal station to which the Laws of Nature *and of Nature's God* entitle them, a decent respect to the opinions of mankind requires that they should declare the causes which impel them to the separation...."

It was in this form, with two pointed references to God, that the Declaration was submitted to Congress. But Congress was not quite satisfied. Although they made many deletions from the final draft and a few other changes in wording, *they insisted upon two insertions*. In the next to the last sentence they made it clear that they were *"appealing to the Supreme Judge of the world for the rectitude of our intentions."* And, in the very last sentence of the Declaration of Independence, they strengthened their affirmation of our dependence on God by adding the words, *"...with a firm reliance on the protection of divine Providence,* we mutually pledge to each other our Lives, our Fortunes, and our sacred Honor."

The Founding Fathers knew that the truths contained in the Declaration were based on an old, old doctrine. They well knew it had come down through the long centuries: that for thousands of years, despite persecution, defection, and obstacles of every sort, the Jews had kept alive the sublime concept that man has an eternal destiny, that he derives his rights from his Creator, and that because of this he has solemn obligations to his fellowmen, in each of whom he should see a child of God. Their view of man's spiritual nature had always been clear-cut. The author of *Genesis*, writing twelve or thirteen centuries before Christ, put it very specifically: *"God created man in His own image.... The Lord God formed man out of the dust of the earth, and breathed into his nostrils the breath of life; and man became a living being"* (Genesis 1:27; 2:7).

God didn't have so to favor us. He could have formed us on the same level as the beasts of the field. Yet precisely because He did make us "living souls" with the gift of understanding and reason, He left us with an obligation to exercise our God-given rights BUT *with an equal opportunity to see that these rights are neither ignored nor abused.*

So far, unfortunately, too many of us have both ignored and abused them. A New York daily not long ago revealed its alarm over this apathy and abuse in words that should strike home to each and every one of us.

"Try this, if you will," it stated. "Go into any group — the more prosperous and fashionable the better the test — and speak of the 'self-evident truth that all men are endowed by their Creator with certain inalienable rights, that among these are life, liberty and the pursuit of happiness.' Say to this group that 'to secure these rights governments are instituted among men.' We venture that you will be startled by the number of people, particularly the younger people, who do not know that you are quoting the Declaration of Independence. And of those who know, a large number will not agree with the philosophy expressed. And of those who agree — and this is the most tragic thing — many will not have the courage to say so."

Ignorance, apathy, abuse... too many of us are lulled into a conviction that the problem will take care of itself.

It will not and it cannot. The only answer is to have more and more bearers of the *truth*, especially in those phases of life which, for better or worse, fashion the destinies of people — education, government, labor and communications (newspapers, magazines, books, radio, television and motion pictures). Put enough people who are fighters for the truth in each of those fields, and the rest will take care of itself.

The Cure: More "Bearers of the Light" — More Christophers!

That is the answer, and there is nothing original about it. It is as old as the hills! As soon as there are more people turning on the lights than there are those turning them off, then the darkness disappears.

Some unknown author put it simply, yet so well: "Such is the irresistible nature of truth, that all it asks, and all it wants, is the liberty of appearing. The sun needs no inscription to distinguish it from darkness."

Even those who have little or no time for religion are beginning to see that now. They are beginning to realize that the evil forces that have risen up over the world in the last few years to crush them, have worked even more furiously to stamp out Christianity because it alone has *the light of Truth;* it alone is the one universal cause that champions man's dignity.

They are beginning to see that all the godless follow one

pattern, namely, to deny or ignore the sacredness of the individual so that the State may become supreme.

What to do about it? It will avail us nothing merely to mumble "incredible," and blindly lash out against our enemies. That is like trying to fight *against* darkness when it would be much more constructive and effective to fight for *light.*

Neither should we think we are too few to make any real progress in solving the enormous problems now confronting us. Time and again throughout history a few have saved the many. If you recall, God Himself was willing to spare whole cities if a handful could be found who were filled with the love of God and the love of man: *"If I find fifty innocent people in the city of Sodom, I will spare the whole place for their sake"* (Genesis 18:26).

Nor should we think that to be Christ-bearers we have to destroy. Emphasis should be on saving. *"I have come not to destroy, but to fulfill"* (Matthew 5:17). The words of Pope St. Gregory in A.D. 597 illustrate this point with all the keen insight of one who clearly saw the way salvation was to be shared with all mankind. Writing to St. Augustine of Canterbury, and instructing him how he was to approach the problem of Christianizing England, Gregory advised him to transform heathen temples into Christian churches rather than to destroy them, and, whenever possible, to adapt heathen practices to the celebration of Christian festivals. *"For,"* declared Gregory, *"he who would ascend a height must mount, not by leaps, but step by step."*

To bring Christ to the world we also must ascend "not by leaps, but step by step." Obviously, we don't have to possess all the saintly virtues to achieve that purpose.

Furthermore, as encouragement to all in working toward a cure, it is no small consolation that to do effective good as a Christopher one does not necessarily have to be brilliant, well-trained, or in high position, for *"God chose what is foolish in the world to shame the wise, the weak of the world to shame the strong"* (1 Corinthians 1:27).

Today there are millions who would thrill to follow in the footsteps of the first apostles, to be twentieth-century apostles, no matter in how small a way. One young woman, for instance, who works in a store in Boston, wrote not long ago that she is trying to do her bit. All she does, as she modestly puts it, is not get "mad" at anybody. When her fellow workers try to taunt her with their disbelief in God, all she does is reply with some friendly quip, such as: "Sure you believe in Him! There's a lot of good in you." And seldom, if ever, has she received a harsh retort to this honest confidence in them.

In another instance, an older woman, who had little education and who made her living sweeping the floors in a department store after it closed in the evening, was so filled with the love of God that she decided to try and get another job where she could meet people and share that love with them; where she might serve, in her own small way, as an instrument of Christ.

With the wisdom which God invariably showers upon "little people" who are anxious to do His will, she transferred to a nearby women's college attended by students from all over the country. She got a job sweeping and cleaning in one of the dormitories, and, as she goes about her daily chores, she makes it her business to meet as many of the young women as she can. Her whole approach is one of loving solicitude for each of them. She doesn't say much, but few students are not touched by her deep faith when she says to one of them, "I suppose lots of folks will tell you there is no God, but I tell you there is! And He loves you — and I pray for you every day at Mass."

These two zealous apostles — and thousands like them all over this land — have caught and are catching the Christopher idea, an idea which is basically missionary. We must saturate our whole society with it, and, by so doing, we may easily change the whole course of history! God is behind us. He will supply His grace in abundance in what may be, for us, the most unusual opportunity since the creation of mankind to recapture the world for Christ. Far from being dismayed, we should realize it is a great time to be alive!

We, The One Million, Have The Answer

In this land today there are probably a million lay persons willing and anxious to play the role of a Christopher in every and all walks of life. And although specially trained workers are essential for the more complex problems, the great pioneer work, the leavening of the multitude with Christian ideals, can be done in the same simple way it was by the early Christians of the catacombs. The one power that accounted for their tremendous success was their consuming love for *all* men, even their worst enemies, in each of whom they saw the image of Christ Himself.

And it is a power which the least of us can have. It is the *cure* for which mankind longs. It should not be forgotten, however, that we are followers of a Crucified One: as He suffered in His love for all mankind, so we must suffer likewise. Mary, His Mother, the *first* bearer of Christ, who brought Him into the world, suffered much. To be a Christ-bearer, a Christopher, must mean sacrifice, loss of time, inconvenience, suffering, misunderstanding, and countless disappointments that truly "try men's souls."

Still the answer is in our hands. For the next twenty or thirty years, or perhaps longer, this nation will play the leading role in world affairs. Which way it will lead depends upon us. If the Christian principles that make our country possible are reawakened in the One Hundred Million who know not the Truth, or have forgotten it, we can lead the world back to Christ.

It is a terrible challenge, but we must face the facts. There is no other way than the way of Christ: *"I am the Way, and the Truth, and the Life*" (John 14:6). If we but strike a spark, that spark, in the Providence of God, may burst into a flame of love which will fire all mankind.

But there is no time to lose. We must show speed. The efforts of even the least among us will be blessed with results that will exceed our wildest dreams.

God willing, we may yet recapture the world for Christ!

It is a great time to be alive!

CHAPTER THREE

Purpose Makes the Difference

"To the glory of God alone!" Such was the inspiring dedication which Johann Sebastian Bach, one of the greatest composers of all time, gave to each of the works which came from his generous heart and gifted pen.

For twenty-seven years he served as director of music at a church in Leipzig, Germany. If he had taken this post simply to earn a living, or to make a name for himself, he would have lived and died unknown, like so many of those who have no interest outside themselves. At best he would have been forgotten, good though his life may have been in its own small way.

But, filled as he was with the love of God and his fellow-man, Bach had only one ambition. That was to serve as an instrument, however unworthy, to reflect the glory of the Most High into the lives of as many of God's children as he could. Little did he dream that because of this inspiring objective he was to draw out of himself a power of composition of such exquisite beauty that, instead of reaching only a few in Leipzig, or Germany, he would reach the world and generations then unborn. And to millions over the earth, he would bring through his magnificent cantatas and oratorios a fleeting glimpse of the majesty of the Creator of all.

That was his *purpose*, his motivation — to love God above

all else and to love his neighbor because he saw in him the image of the Almighty.

Bach's whole life was a demonstration of the *power* of Christian love, and not a few people have recognized that. But, strangely enough, one of the greatest testimonials to the efficacy of that power came, not from an historian, a feature writer or an ecclesiastic, but from Anatole Lunacharsky, former Commissar of Education in the U.S.S.R.

"We hate Christianity and Christians," this Communist proclaimed in 1935. "Even the best of them must be considered our worst enemies. They preach love of one's neighbor and mercy, which is contrary to our principles. *Christian love is an obstacle to the development of the revolution.* Down with love of our neighbor! What we want is hatred. We must know how to hate. Only thus will we conquer the universe!" (Quoted in *Izvestia*)

Note well the significance of that statement. *"Christian love is an obstacle to the development of the revolution."* It illustrates, as much as words possibly can, the undeniable fact that only those with a burning love, or a burning hatred, have a cause that is greater than themselves. They alone can change the world for better or for worse. The "in-betweeners" accomplish little or nothing.

For those who live only for themselves, even Christ Himself has small regard: *"I wish that you were either hot or cold, but because you are lukewarm and neither cold nor hot, I am about to spit you out of My mouth"* (Revelation 3:15).

Each of us has to have a sense of dedication, a sense of sacrifice that will go beyond ourselves.

If those who spread confusion have found in a method borrowed from Christianity a spirit of purpose, we have not the slightest excuse for neglecting that method a day longer. In every home, church and school, in business, government, education and the writing fields, our people must constantly be inspired to play a personal part as missioners in *changing the world for the better*. And in doing this, not only will the inspiration touch the best that is in them and strike a responsive chord, but it will render a tremendous service to humanity.

The genuineness and sincerity of our love of people is not measured by academic attitudes, by passing resolutions, by meeting once a month and complaining about conditions in the world and then coming back a month later to complain some more. Mere lip service is almost the equivalent of nothing at all.

Paul's Driving Purpose

To love your neighbor as yourself means *doing* for others as we would *do* for ourselves, regardless of the time spent, inconvenience involved, even real suffering itself sometimes endured. In this, we might well take to heart the example of the Apostle Paul. Few in history have been driven more by this purpose than was he. Literally and figuratively, he was consumed with the burning desire to share his love of Christ with anyone and everyone. One of the most striking instances of his tender solicitude and of how tactfully considerate he could be in his approach is eloquently evident in an account of an experience he had in Greece.

While waiting in Athens for his coworkers to join him, no one would have blamed him if he had taken time off to rest since he planned to be there only a few days. Yet he did nothing of the kind, because to give way to his comfort would have been to think only of himself. He felt an *obligation* to the Athenians and, as the Scripture narrates, *"He was deeply distressed to see that the city was full of idols"* (Acts 17:16).

Even though it could only be a passing effort, he decided not to remain aloof. Making his way to the business center, to the market place, where he would come in direct contact with the men of Athens, he began to strike up conversations with all whom he met. They regarded him as a meddler, but that didn't bother him for he was used to such a reception. One with the loving purpose which inflamed Paul pays little heed to any expression of disdain or contempt. He kept moving deeper and deeper into their midst, until they *had* to pay attention to him. Finally, they decided to give him a public hearing and invited him to the Areopagus.

His opening words reveal the loving heart and soul of Paul. They are a masterpiece of tender regard for others who had beliefs very much opposed to his own, yet show that in no way did he compromise with them. One with less tact or less farsightedness could easily have upbraided them for being *"given over to idolatry,"* but not Paul! From the very start he wins them by saying, *"Men of Athens, I see how extremely religious you are in every way,"* referring to the idols which adorned the temple. Then quickly he gets to the point with another apt remark which distinguishes, yet neither cuts nor hurts.

Noticing one altar not erected to any god in particular but rather serving the purpose of being useful for new gods for whom no other altar could be found, Paul continues:

"As I went through the city and looked carefully at the objects of your worship, I found among them an altar with the inscription, 'To an unknown god.' What therefore you worship as unknown, this I proclaim to you. The God Who made the world and everything in it, He Who is Lord of heaven and earth, does not live in shrines made by human hands, nor is He served by human hands, as though He needed anything, since He Himself gives to all mortals life and breath and all we have. From one ancestor He made all nations to inhabit the whole earth."

And he adds still another expression of his love for these men of Athens, so intent is he on emphasizing similarities, not differences. After saying, *"He is not far from any one of us; for 'In Him we live, and move, and have our being',"* he concludes with the reminder that some among them have already said that very thing: *"Even some of your poets have told us,"* he says, *"'For we, too, are His offspring'."*

The Aim of Every Christopher

It should be the constant goal of every Christopher to follow this pattern of approach laid down by Paul in the first recorded talk on Christianity given in Europe. In the eleven sentences that make up his brief address are numerous lessons from which we can profit, but three in particular have a special meaning for one who is a "bearer of Christ":

1. The whole of Paul's motivation was *love* of the Athenians even though they were "given over to idolatry." He felt that the love of Christ belonged to them as much as to himself. It was his job to adapt himself to them, not to expect them to conform to him. He strove hard not to offend. He was not merely trying to prove how wrong were they and how right was he. He was not out to "beat them down" nor to hurt them in any way. On the contrary, he went to extraordinary lengths to single out every possible point of agreement. He went to them — he did *not* wait for them to come to him. Anyone who has a true love of people will do just that.

2. Another simple truth Paul stressed was *the existence of a personal God* Who has spoken to the world and on Whom the world depends.

That is the one immutable truth a Christopher who is steeped in a genuine love of people will strive incessantly to bring to all. It is the truth upon which mankind must base all hope for a better world. It is the truth that the Founders of our country reverently and repeatedly affirmed in the Declaration of Independence.

In stressing this one truth, Paul did not intimate this was all of religion, but he did lay down most emphatically, though so simply, the fact that this was the one cornerstone upon which all else depends. And it is this cornerstone that all forms of materialism and totalitarianism relentlessly oppose and seek to destroy. Therefore, it should be the one truth above all others that a Christopher strives to carry into every phase of public and private life.

3. While Paul made very few converts from this talk — only "Dionysius, Damaris and others with them" — he was primarily interested in doing far more than winning a handful of followers. He didn't measure success by the number who went the full way with him. He was out to reach everybody, no matter how they received his message. He was doing exactly what Christ commanded. He was going to "all men," into the "highways" as well as the "byways." And he knew full well that he was planting seeds which would blossom later; that he was leavening the multitude; that, because he had taken the trouble to go into the marketplace of Athens as the first Christ-bearer to enter there, he had brought countless numbers at least one step closer to Christ.

The true Christopher, motivated by love of all people for love of God, is continually trying to reach the many, not merely the few. The multitude, not merely a single individual. And that is why, like Paul, a Christ-bearer goes *where people are* — into the marketplaces, into the four great spheres that vitally influence, for better or worse, the great mass of humanity. He or she goes into *the educational field, government, labor-management relations, the writing field* (press, radio, television, motion pictures, books, and magazines).

In other words, the Christopher gets out of his own little world and into the big world, a world which will be run either by those who hate Christ or who know Him not, or by those who dedicate themselves to bringing mankind back to "the Way, the Truth, and the Life."

Every Christopher recognizes that fact. In their own perverted way, so do the godless. The "in-betweeners" apparently do not — those otherwise good people who, because of their apathy, are making a negligible impact on the basic problems that convulse our nation and the world. They pretend to be so absorbed in saving their own souls as to justify giving scarcely a passing thought to the salvation of their neighbors. They are solicitous for everything concerning their own personal security, but seldom lift a finger in behalf of the economic security of the hundreds of millions all over the earth who often turn in desperation, as to their only hope of securing social justice, to those who champion violence and even death.

Everyone should have a reasonable interest in good housing, good food, good clothing, and other personal advantages. The "in-betweeners," however, so distort this interest that they rarely get beyond taking care of themselves. Rarely do they devote time and energy to providing the personal leadership now so urgently needed to win for the great masses of mankind not convenience or luxuries, but the bare necessities of life which God intends as their minimum right.

The Overemphasis on Self

Parents, directors and teachers too often are so preoccupied with protecting the young that they overemphasize self-preservation, self-sanctification, self-development, and self-enjoyment. Without intending any harm, they give their children the impression they have only one mission in life — to take care of themselves. Little do they realize this is only part of Christianity; that by failing to pass on the fullness of Christ's message they are clipping the wings of their own youngsters, fencing them in, depriving them of the more abundant and interesting life that God meant them to have. And in so many instances, they are heading for the monotony, the frustration, even the tragedy which is the inevitable result of concentration on self.

More often than not, they go through life hitting on only one or two cylinders when they could be driving ahead on all eight;

they go through the years leading a drab, dull, even if harmless existence; scarcely conscious they have buried the talents God has given them. They live and die, never once realizing that Christ did *not* say to love God and self only — that is a primary and essential foundation, to be sure, but is only part of Christianity. The fullness of Christianity is to love others — all people. How much? Christ's standard admits of no evasion: "As yourself." The attitude of "God and myself," therefore, is not enough. It must be "God, myself, and everybody else."

The tragic story of Germany when the Nazis first began to come into power cannot be retold too often. If the *good* German people had followed that admonition of Christ and thought as much of others as they did of themselves, Hitler would never have succeeded in seizing power.

Where Europe failed, however, we can succeed! For us there is still *hope* — *refreshing hope* — that it will not take much to rectify and remove the major ills that still plague mankind. And this can be done without tearing down or destroying anything.

All that is necessary is to extend, to continue, to develop, in each individual that fullness of true love, not only for God and self, but for others as well, that Christ laid down as the indispensable foundation of lasting peace. Moreover, it can be done quickly because this purpose taps a force for good that is deep within every human heart, a force that is ready and waiting to plunge in a practical, timely way into action capable of overcoming every obstacle.

There are numerous places to practice and perfect this love of others. One of the best places to start is in the home, especially when circumstances are difficult, perhaps even seemingly hopeless. Such action — Christopher action — will arrest much of the divorce, the juvenile delinquency, the general breakdown of morale that is creeping steadily into millions of homes as love of one another diminishes and the spirit of "every man for himself" begins to dominate with tragic results.

Sometimes tensions appear near the surface, reflected in quiet desperation, in accumulated failures, frustration and worry. But in numerous other instances, they break out violently, like flames from a smoldering pile of rubbish. To verify this you have only to pick up the daily newspapers and read the headlines of those extreme cases which are becoming more and more prevalent: "Torture Suspect Confesses," "Mother Stabs Infant to Death," "Despondent Couple Leap From Bridge."

In all of these cases the background is the same. These are the unhappy mortals who are sick of their jobs, sick of their families and friends, sick of their very lives.

Yet the happy hope in all this dark picture is that millions of Americans who are on the brink of mental and emotional disaster can be guided toward self-salvation simply by convincing them to "wake up and live" — to use to the utmost the fullness of their lives which God intended to be their due. To get out of themselves, and their real or imagined troubles by helping others to help themselves.

One mother instilled this love of neighbor into her children in season and out. But she went further. In her last will and testament she left far more than her worldly possessions. She bequeathed to them a priceless legacy that well sums up the Christlike objective of her life:

"Love one another. Hold fast to that whether you understand one another or not. And remember nothing really matters except loving God and others over the whole world as far as you can reach."

True Love Knows No Boundaries

It is of the essence of true love of others that it seeks to diffuse itself, that it knows no boundaries, that it stirs you to share it and spread it "over the world as far as you can reach." It is this all-inclusive love that sustains and furnishes the driving power for one who wishes to be a lifetime Christopher. It is a constant reminder that the world itself will be better off because he or she has lived in it.

True love of others is the encouraging reminder to the Christ-bearer that he or she is working on the side of the fundamental goodness which the Creator of all has imbedded deep in the heart and soul of each and every human being. The most hateful person in the world wants to be loved. The worst criminal often takes great pains to appear as a respectable citizen, insisting that others be honest with him. The most immoral of men cautiously guards the dignity of his wife and children.

No matter to what lengths people go to root out of their fellowmen that sense of decency which distinguishes man from the brute animal, they never completely succeed. Some remnants always remain, awaiting development. There is always hope, even in the worst of people.

All we need do to make that fact real in our lives is to conduct a little experiment in self-examination of our relations to the physical world around us. When we do, we will come to realize that the Hand of God cradles the whole human race in loving solicitude.

Anyone who is fixed with a Christ-like purpose — a Christopher purpose — and who wants to reach all people will see the wisdom of using three methods recommended by our Lord Himself. If you love your fellow men and women, you will:

1. Pray for them.
2. Go to them.
3. Teach them.

Praying for All

This is an effective method of Christopher participation open to one and all. It is one of the easiest ways to grow in love of all people. Pray especially for those for whom few, if any, pray — for the confused, the evil, even the hateful. When you board a plane or get on a bus, go to a theater or to a football or baseball game, or down to the beach, say a passing prayer for everyone there. Eternity has begun for each individual present, no matter how little they know or think about it. When you pick up the morning paper and scan the death notices, let them be a reminder to offer a brief prayer for all who have died the world over during the preceding twenty-four hours.

The tendency on the part of most of us is to restrict our prayers to our own selfish interests, overlooking the far greater needs of the millions in our own country, for example, who are drifting farther and farther away from Christ. "Love your neighbor as yourself" certainly means to pray as much for others as one does for self. No matter how busy you are or what your position in life may be, whether you are old or young, with a college degree or barely out of kindergarten, you can get in a daily prayer for the billion and more souls throughout the world who have yet to hear that Jesus Christ was born, lived, and died for each of us, nearly two thousand years ago. You can pray for the millions who are hungry or starving and who are not allowed to exercise their God-given human rights and liberties.

Pray each day for your government. If enough Americans do this, it will be a powerful step in the right direction. One shopkeeper sets aside a portion of each day to pray that God may guide individual officials in Washington in fulfilling their important tasks wisely and fearlessly. Such prayer will increase your interest in taking other positive measures to see that all of us have the best possible government. You will actively participate in saving your country (and the world itself) as others are active in attempting to wreck it. No matter how remote you may feel, even if you are bed-ridden, you can play a vital role.

By Going

Our Lord could not have been more insistent on this point. Over and over again He told His followers to *"go"* and keep *"going,"* without ceasing, into the midst of all men the world over. And lest anyone think He was generalizing, here are His words, and they are most specific: *"Go out to all the world and proclaim the good news to the whole of creation"* (Mark 16:15).

Thank God this command was taken to heart by some, otherwise mankind might still be groping in deeper darkness than that which grips us now. The early Christians didn't sit in the catacombs, complaining about the ruthlessness of the Romans. They realized it was their one big job to go to them in every possible way, with the conviction that Christ died for them also and that His love belonged likewise to them. As slaves, into kitchens, onto farms, into trading houses and even into the army — in any and every capacity — they *went.*

They could easily have said, *"They didn't want us,"* or *"It's too hard,"* or *"I must get paid more than that."* They did just the opposite. They continued to go in the face of the most frightful odds. In imitation of Christ's loving purpose, they endured imprisonment, scourging, ridicule, and death by the sword, by fire, by being thrown to wild beasts. And their terrible sufferings were not in vain. Without destroying anything, they eventually won — won by "going" and by "loving" even those who drained the very life blood out of them.

Today the task is much easier; but the followers of Christ, while totaling hundreds of millions over the earth, have ceased to *go* except in far too few numbers. Once that trend is reversed and large numbers of people are once more *going* with Christ's love and peace into every phase of activity, into the highways as well as the byways, then and then only will there be a substantial change for the better.

Later chapters will include detailed accounts of the four important fields into which Christophers are urged to *go*, because, through them, most of humanity is affected for good or evil, for better or worse. But no matter in what capacity he or she *goes*, any follower of Christ can do at least one of the thousands of possible things to bring Him into the marketplace. Where there's a will there's a way!

For example, a young mother, still suffering from the effects of tuberculosis, frequently manages to get over to any who chance to cross her path an understanding of and a sympathy for some fundamental Christian truth. A Wall Street broker has a special hobby of approaching individually any who belong to no church, tactfully discussing some basic Christian doctrine and then passing on a piece of literature for later reading. Nearly every one of the hundreds contacted on this person-to-person basis has been most receptive and even grateful that he bothered.

Others are taking literally the command of Christ to *go*. They are devoting any time they can spare from home or work to *going* with a Christopher purpose into clubs, parent-teacher associations, civic and welfare groups, food and housing movements, scout work, and any number of other endeavors that affect the general public and therefore need the leaven of Christ's Truth to keep them functioning for the good of all.

By Teaching

Christophers can do something to carry the teachings of Christ to the world. All of us have at least an obligation to offer to others and to share with them the truths given us by Christ.

All we have to do is play the role of messengers. God could have arranged to have this done entirely by angels, but the fact is that He did not. He willed that men should be saved through their fellowmen. All He asks us to do is to pass along, to distribute, the simple, eternal fundamentals that are the basis of happiness for mankind in this life and in the life to come. He assured us He would always provide us with an abundance of help from on high, that we would not work alone. The more we fulfill this noble role, the more we can say with Christ: *"For this was I was born, and for this I came into the world, to testify to the truth"* (John 18:37).

A young man doing excellent Christopher work specializes, as all Christophers should, in reaching those in whom no one else is interested — the weak rather than the strong, the spiritually hungry rather than those who have all the advantages of life at their disposal. In business, at parties, on trains, in taxis, on the street, with people in trouble, with the sick, the poor, with government officials, his every act is a prayer. He tries to fulfill the Master's command to "Love your neighbor as yourself." And because he has such a zealous love for others, friendly and hostile, he has drawn thousands a little closer to God. A nonreligious acquaintance of his recently confided to a friend, "I didn't know people existed with the love of God in their heart which that boy has."

In each of these instances and in thousands of others, truth, while it is divine, is dispensed in *a human* way, as it will always be. Academic theories leave most people cold. They are fed up with more and more housing plans. What they want are homes. Hungry people are not stirred up by recipes. They are looking for food.

Love of God as well as others is something active and dynamic, not a treasure to be hidden or discussed in vague terms. When each of us stands before God in final judgment, He will not ask how well dressed we were, how much money we made, how many trips we took, how much fame or glory we won for ourselves. But He will ask us — and our eternity will depend on the answer — what each of us did in His name for others.

The Selfish — And the Selfless

He who recognizes the Divine Image in those around him and therefore strives to help them will find himself among those answering the eternal invitation of Christ: *"Come, you who are blessed by My Father, inherit the kingdom prepared for you from the foundation of the world"* (Matthew 25:34). But he who has lived only for himself will hear the very opposite: *"You who are accursed, depart from Me into the eternal fire prepared for the devil and his angels; for I was hungry and you gave Me no food; I was thirsty and you gave Me nothing to drink. I was a stranger, and you did not welcome Me; naked and you did not give Me clothing; sick and in prison, and you did not visit Me"* (Matthew 25:41-43).

To the protest that will invariably come from those so charged, that they would certainly have ministered to Christ if they had even seen Him "hungry or thirsty, or a stranger, or naked, or sick, or in prison," the answer of Christ will be that standard by which He dignifies *every* human being: *"Just as you did not do it to one of the least of these, you did not do it to Me"* (Matthew 25:45).

Long before they die, those who disregard others in furthering their own selfish interests begin to pay the penalty. They are never completely at peace. No matter how much of this world's goods they may possess, they seem forever ill at ease, restless, dissatisfied never to have caught up with the rainbow they are pursuing. In their lives the lack of purpose outside themselves has a depressing reaction on all that is best in them. On their faces and in their eyes there is little luster or gleam. Inside them, something seems to have died.

Those, however, whose lives are motivated with the vital purpose of doing all they can for others, actually begin to live some of their heaven on earth. Nothing daunts them. They develop a gaiety of heart that carries them through the most trying circumstances. They stay young in spirit. They quickly learn that thoroughness is the quality of true love, of true charity for others. With St. Paul they can say *"Love is patient; love is kind; love is not envious or boastful or arrogant or rude. It does not insist on its own way; it is not irritable or resentful; it does not rejoice in wrongdoing, but rejoices in the truth. It bears all things, believes all things, hopes all things, endures all things."* (1 Corinthians 13:4-7).

As you grow in this love for others, you will find your horizons expanding and your own power increasing. Even your sense of proportion will grow as you take yourself less seriously and others more seriously. You will learn how to disagree without being disagreeable. You will become more approachable. You will better understand why *all people* want to be truly loved, and not just tolerated. You will emphasize more and more the good side of even the worst of people; and you will recognize, as a result, the far-reaching significance of Christ's words: *"Love your enemies, do good to those who hate you, bless those who curse you, and pray for those who insult you"* (Luke 6:27-28).

Christ doesn't want you to be a Casper Milquetoast, just realistic and appreciative of the simple fact that some hate only because they lack that precious quality of love. In true solicitude for them, as a Christopher, you can do something positive and constructive by supplying that lack, filling up that void, by sharing your own love.

You will be, in short, *another* Christ. And, more and more, you will be able to say with the Apostle Paul, *"It is no longer I who live, but it is Christ who lives in me"* (Galatians 2:20).

This sublime motivation, this loving purpose will distinguish you who seriously strive to bring Christ into the marketplace.

Because of this dedication to a cause, welling up within you will be a driving power which pushes through all obstacles, with patience and kindness. More and more you will be inflamed with a fire which warms but does not burn. Everything you say or do will reflect that devotion, loyalty, and quiet enthusiasm which is seldom, if ever, the happy lot of those whose only cause is themselves.

A remarkable transformation will take place in you, and often surprisingly quickly, once you make within yourself the simple adjustment from dull, narrow concentration on self, to the stimulating, vitalizing interest and concern in the general good of all. From having been unaware of anything beyond your own little, self-contained sphere, you will become a Christopher stepping out into the mainstream of life, into the thick of things. By God's help, you will be forever buoyed up with the knowledge that the world itself is at least a tiny bit the better because you are in it.

Where, in the past, your approach to life was one of selfish timidity and fearful caution, you will find yourself charged with Christ's daring, bold, yet prudent "launching out," yet never reckless. From being half-hearted in most things, you will become wholehearted in all things. Instead of consulting first your own personal convenience before doing anything for anyone else, you will become lovingly absorbed in doing everything and anything for others. Where, previously, the slightest pretext could deflect or discourage you, nothing now will daunt your determination and sense of follow-through.

Invariably you will develop an inner warmth which manifests itself in an abiding sense of humor even in the midst of the most trying circumstances. You invariably will reflect in everything you do a Christopher concern for all. Naturally you will make mistakes. But you will always retain enough sense of proportion to laugh at yourself. Your never-say-die spirit will give courage to everyone you meet. Because you are eternally hopeful, you will often bring new light and new hope into the drab lives of those who have no cause beyond themselves — and who, consequently, have no sparkle either for themselves or for others.

And no matter what your limitations are, your noble purpose and your deep and satisfying conviction that, by God's grace, you can be an instrument in bringing Him to others and others to Him will develop in you an ever-increasing imagination and enterprise which constantly leads you on to new and greater heights. Too, this healthy, divine discontent will increase within you a growing resourcefulness, and alertness, a keenness of observation, and a capacity for work which might have lain dormant and undeveloped if the greater cause had not lifted you out of all the depressing smallness and self-torture of concentrating only on self.

More literally than anyone else, you will experience the real *joy of living*. Life itself will take on a new and exhilarating meaning. You will have the fun and thrill of knowing that, in however small a measure, you are building, not destroying; spreading love, not hate; light, not darkness. You will be fulfilling, in the most literal sense and to the fullest measure possible, the purpose for which you were created: to *love God above all things and your neighbor as yourself.*

CHAPTER FOUR

Education

Ideas Determine the Future

"All he ever talks about is learning enough to graduate so he can go out and make some money!" The speaker, a brown-eyed youth with a shock of bushy black hair, planted himself squarely in front of a dark-complexioned boy with serious eyes and a tight expression around the corners of his mouth. As he mentally gathered himself for another outburst, another in the group of boys standing outside a public high school in the heart of New York's East Side spoke up.

"Leave him alone, Al," he said quickly. "Maybe he doesn't know any better."

"Maybe — maybe not," came back the disgruntled reply. "But if he could see the letters my father gets from the old country, telling us what a break we've got living over here where we can do what we want, he'd quit that money stuff. Money isn't everything!"

"Cut it out, Al," the object of the outburst broke in. "Don't get sore."

"I'm not sore — just fed up, up to here." The first boy drew an imaginary line under his chin with a grimy forefinger. "The sooner you and others like you find out we've got to do like my father says — have God some place in our setup — the better off things will be around here."

An amazing incident? Agreed. But amazing as it was, it actually happened. A Christopher, a public school teacher, was lucky enough to see and hear what took place from behind the wheel of her parked car a few feet away. As best she could, she jotted down what she saw and heard and passed it on to us. What struck her, and us, more than anything else, however, was the one remark: "…have God some place in our setup." It was a surprising remark, and it is one seldom made by the youth in our schools. In fact, the typical reply to the question, "What are you studying for?" is usually summed up in the words, "To get a job and make some money." Nothing more.

It is the answer given by ninety-five out of every hundred of the best young American people, regardless of whether their grammar is all it should be or whether they use the language of the neighborhoods in which they live.

Of course money is needed to conduct normal lives, that is understood. But money is not the be-all and end-all of our existence. It is the overemphasis on money and on other material things that points up one significant fact that few people seem to recognize. It is that education in America right now is going through a process of de-spiritualization that will leave it without a sense of morality. And if there is no morality, there can be no law other than that of force.

Consider these words of the great poet, John Milton, written three hundred years ago:

"The end of learning is to repair the ruins of our first parents by regaining to know God aright, and out of that knowledge to love Him, to imitate Him, to be like Him, as we may the nearest by possessing our souls of true virtue, which being united to heavenly grace of faith makes up the highest perfection."

The spiritual vacuum in America today is the fruit of an educational policy which for years has ignored God. If there is to be a clearer concept of morality we must rely in most schools on literature, English, foreign languages, mathematics, natural science and social science — in short, on *education* — to develop the concept that this is a universe founded upon law, *the law of God!* We must impress upon our youth that the violations of that law carry consequences quite apart from human imposition.

The Function of Education

Education must train the human will along with the intellect. It must produce a "free man." This is the basic education which our Founding Fathers urged as needed for the perpetuation of the Republic.

Education — good education — must point out, teach, and emphasize most convincingly that "man shall not live by bread alone." It must be dedicated to the proposition, *"For what good would it do a man to gain the whole world, but lose his own soul?"* (Matthew 16:26).

Education must stress one fundamental fact which alone makes social living possible: man must be educated for his ultimate goal in life, the end for which he was created — to know, love, and serve God and to be happy with Him in the life to come.

Education must stand for liberty to exercise the rights God has given us, otherwise it will yield to tyranny. The truest education produces a self-disciplined individual, recognizing the existence of a personal God to Whom he or she will one day be accountable.

Our Obligation

The time has come — indeed, the hour is late, though not too late, thank God — to bring back once more into our classrooms these and other Christian truths which form the basis of our existence and of the existence of the United States of America.

Not for one moment should it be forgotten that a change for the better will take place only when, as, and if those who believe in God and therefore have a more serious responsibility — Protestants, Jews, and Catholics alike — really interest themselves in the millions of young Americans now in our schools. To abandon these, your very own, to the evil concern of those whose gospel is hate and materialism is to let go by default your children's future and the future of the greatest democracy the world has ever known.

You people of strong, solid values — teachers, parents, and even students — must take back into your hands the positive conduct of sound education. As Christophers, you must seize the personal initiative which can restore to the marketplace the Christian heritage of America.

You must no longer neglect to provide your share of good teachers. You must no longer give way to parental apathy but show instead an active and continuing concern in seeing that the policies and administration of all schools are strengthening America, not weakening it. You must not hide your light under a bushel while an energetic minority who deny God and the basic concept of American life are shouting their doctrine of darkness from the housetops, from the classroom and the campus, from the study clubs and the vocational guidance centers.

In short, as American citizens and taxpayers, not only do you have the right, but a serious obligation as well, to see that all schools supported by taxes, whether they be city, county, or state, are manned by healthy minded Americans, not by those who would destroy our very civilization.

Classification of the Academic Field

To help orientate those Christ-bearers who wish to do something as individuals in bringing education back to the original purpose for which it was intended — to train the soul along with the intellect — a very brief classification of the entire academic field is of first importance.

Education may be broken down in a variety of ways: elementary, intermediate, and advanced; parochial and nonsectarian; formal and informal; child and adult.

For our purpose of helping orientate Christophers who wish to do something as individuals in the educational field, the subject can be divided under three main headings: the teacher, the parent, and the student.

The Teacher

The teacher's main responsibility is the classroom. He or she is one of the great channels whereby the heritage and traditions of a civilization are transmitted to the young whose habits, ideas and way of life will determine the course of our national and world future. There can be no greater work for anyone for, as Cicero said, "What nobler employment or more valuable to the state, than that of the man who instructs the rising generation?"

Man's ascent through the ages has been long and hard, and at each step he has accumulated new knowledge, about things, about people, about the relationship of men, one to the other, in accordance with the Divine Plan. This sum total of our wisdom is in our hands today. The teacher hands the keeping of this world to those whom he or she instructs. It is doubly important that those who guide the thinking of the carefree student of today and make of him the responsible citizen of tomorrow should be men and women of sound ideas. Never forget: what is in the teacher's head and heart passes into the minds of the young!

To be a teacher is to have a great mission in life. The instructor of mathematics who shows how to solve a simple equation or how to bisect an angle, the teacher of chemistry who explains how to break water down into its component parts of oxygen and hydrogen, the teacher of domestic science who teaches a student how to make a home more attractive or a meal more edible — all these transmit certain branches of our accumulated knowledge.

Although none of these or allied subjects directly influence the moral and spiritual thinking, indirectly they can be a means of doing so. Just by being in any of these positions, a Christopher takes the place of someone who may be materialistic or subversive. This one fact is most important, for in after-class discussions when children mull over other subjects besides the one in which they have just been instructed, or in teacher associations and parent-teacher groups, the teacher can and should take a leading part in helping mold opinion on all phases of the educational field. This molding involves, as it should, the moral and spiritual side of education as well as the purely intellectual.

Right in the classroom, however, certain subjects do provide a direct opportunity for teaching youngsters how to live in accordance with the moral precepts which are based on the laws of God. The teaching of history offers an excellent chance to inform young men and women of the great struggles for those God-given rights that characterize our Western civilization in particular; in other words, the fight to preserve, as the columnist Walter Lippmann puts it, "the religious tradition of the West."

In the study of literature, great writings can be traced to the growth of those selfsame ideas and ideals which helped make our democratic way of life and brought men and women from slavery to freedom.

Economics — the science that treats of the development of natural resources or the production, preservation and distribution of wealth and methods of living well, for the state, the family, and the individual — provides an excellent background for the examination of a just economy based on God's commandments which apply equally to both employer and employee: to treat one another as you yourself would be treated.

The more advanced courses in civics, political science, comparative government, survey of civilization, philosophy, science and social science can all serve a very positive purpose: to establish man in the proper relationship to his neighbor, remembering that all are the children of God. If the courses fail to do this, or do it badly, the logical question to ask is why are they taught at all?

The very basis of our society involves the recognition and proper use of the rights and responsibilities we receive from God. And, as the Declaration of Independence points out, "To secure these rights, governments are instituted among men."

The greatest sins in our modern teaching are the failure, on one hand, to teach democracy as a creative and dynamic force; and the deliberate attempt, now too long prevalent, to weave warped interpretations into the original concept of what democracy means and of the Source — God — of its very existence.

Without a doubt, right at this moment the crisis in our education can be accelerated to continue our downward descent into the darkness of totalitarianism, or it can be stopped and turned upwards to reflect the will of our Creator by the action of those who have the truth and are willing to share it with their fellowmen; who are willing to help their neighbors and their neighbors' children become better citizens, worthy of the God-given heritage that was so dearly won for them by the founders of our country who pledged their all to make their dream of democracy come true.

George Washington, in a letter to the Hebrew Congregation in Newport, Rhode Island, set forth a principle of which Americans in particular should well be proud, "a policy worthy of imitation," that shines like a beacon light of guidance and hope for all the peoples of the world to follow.

"The citizens of the United States of America," he said, "have a right to applaud themselves for having given to mankind examples of an enlarged and liberal policy; a policy worthy of imitation. All possess alike liberty of conscience and immunities of citizenship. It is now no more that toleration is spoken of, as if it were by indulgence of one class of people, that another enjoyed the exercise of their inherent natural rights. For happily, the Government of the United States, which gives to bigotry no sanction, to persecution no assistance, requires only that they who live under its protection, should demean themselves as good citizens."

The first responsibility of the Christopher who chooses teaching as a career is that of conveying these and other great American truths to the new generation of citizens. More than that, however, the teacher is, or should be, a community figure much respected by the young, a parent substitute for many hours during the day, a counsellor, a companion, an individual worthy of the highest regard. For that reason alone the teacher becomes a figure to imitate and emulate.

By the same token it places on him or her a duty which involves personal deportment as well as civic interest. The voice of the teacher must be heard in the councils of the township, in the press, in public gatherings, in the various group institutions established for mutual help and improvement. In short, the teacher's day should not end with the classroom. People are guided not only by what we say, but also by what we do. And the teacher is in an unusually opportune position to set a pattern of healthy behavior by his or her individual example.

Some teachers in this country are members of trade unions. Teachers who are members of unions must be something more than mere dues-payers; they must be active members. Because too many members of some teachers' union locals have merely affiliated and let it go at that, active minorities with their own strong agendas have been able to capture the leadership of the organization. Their strength, however, lies only in the weakness of those who have the *truth* but who surrender leadership by default.

What is true of some branches of the unions of which teachers are members is true also of many branches of parent-teacher associations, and consideration of these groups brings us to the second of the three main headings into which, as regards individual effort, the entire educational field is divided.

The Parent

Since both parent and teacher are interested in the development of the child, then both teacher and parent should have a chance to meet and jointly discuss the training of the child. But again, the whole relationship can be twisted and perverted if the good people allow the *doers of evil* to do all the attending of PTA meetings, all the talking, all the organizing, all the directing.

That this unfortunate state of affairs has come to pass is borne out by reports coming in from all over the country of parents losing interest in PTA because those who live in the darkness have been more zealous in promoting their false doctrines than have the bearers of light in standing up and proclaiming the truth.

The Christopher — whether parent or teacher — belongs in the thick of things! Absence and apathy on the part of both teacher and parent merely increases the percentage of the irrational at PTA and kindred group meetings. Remember the words of Paul: *"Do not be overcome by evil, but overcome evil with good"* (Romans 12:21).

Another way the parent can exercise direct concern with education is through interest and action in the election of local school boards. These local boards of education help to select books, draft curricula, and supervise in many cases the choice of teachers.

A third avenue of parent participation is in classes for adults. Sometimes these are regular, formal classes; often they are just a series of lectures or an occasional forum. Yet every time, and in varying degrees, they all help to shape the attitudes of the community.

There is a fourth way parents can be extremely helpful in lifting the entire educational system to a higher plane. That is to leave no stone unturned in getting the better-qualified Americans (who, thank God, still constitute the majority of teachers) to reverse the trend away from a teaching career and get back into the thick of things. *This is most important.*

Every effort must be made to provide better pay for teachers, but millions of students must not be abandoned in the meanwhile. It must be possible — please God, it will be possible — to find enough men and women who, fired with the love of Christ, are willing to put up with all the self-sacrifice that a life of teaching entails in order to restore to the marketplace the Christian values upon which our country is founded.

It Is Being Done!

The best proof that this can be done is that many, given only the slightest encouragement, are taking up either teaching careers or positions associated with the educational field, not for what they can "take out," but for what they can "put in." They have caught the Christopher point of view!

One woman who had transferred from a teaching post in a high school to a commercial concern for higher pay recently returned to the classroom — because she came to realize that even though she was only one of hundreds of thousands of teachers, nevertheless she could, by patient persistence, do much that would leave the world better than she found it.

A young man was so concerned, while in college, with the perverted slant being given to the subject of *history,* both ancient and modern, that after receiving his diploma he continued his postgraduate studies with a teaching career in this subject as his goal. He is now an instructor in his specialty in a large western university.

A young woman shifted from a secretarial job with a business firm to become assistant to the head of a department of a well-known university. All sorts of obstacles were placed in her path in an attempt to discourage her, but that only spurred her on the more. She became increasingly convinced that people like herself should forsake their own little worlds and petty comforts and get "into the fight" for *good* with the same determination that others were showing in the fight for evil.

She got the job. Now, in many different ways, she influences the teaching of thousands of students.

At one well-known boys' school there is a teacher who went there with a specific purpose in mind. Familiar with the background of the neighborhood in which the school is situated, he was painfully aware of the lack of spiritual concepts of the families in the area where education was concerned. This condition — passed on to their children — was brought home to him very pointedly one day in class when a young student, hearing him expound on the need for spiritual values in everyday living, exclaimed, "Gee, sir, don't tell us you believe in that tripe!"

It was a hard pill to swallow, but this teacher didn't lose his temper. Instead, kindly but firmly, he has kept hammering away at his beliefs and has had the satisfaction of having more than one boy come up to him and tell him they were beginning to see "daylight" at last.

A superintendent of schools in one of the New England states has remained at his post despite many flattering offers to enter business. "It isn't the easiest thing in the world meeting the expenses of a large family with what I make, especially when I could earn a lot of money if I got out of the educational field," this man told us recently. "But I've made up my mind to stay where I am. The good I can do in helping train young people in sound principles more than makes up for what I lose financially."

For people like these, and millions more like them, there are other tremendous opportunities to put into daily practice the Christopher ideal.

The Student

Individually, the *student* can find four different fields in which his or her chance to be a Christopher is unexcelled. They are the classroom, the school club, the campus (and campus activities), and student movements.

In the *classroom* many subjects lend themselves to teaching through pupil participation and discussion. Student participation in shaping classroom opinion, however, should not degenerate into an endless and annoying repetition of hackneyed phrases because that, for a Christopher, will defeat your very purpose. The student must gain the respect of fellow classmates by his or her scholarliness. The healthy Christopher point of view must flow from the general discussion and not be stuck on to the end of it like a campaign sticker or an envelope. Once again, to repeat Christ's admonition, *"Be as wise as serpents and as innocent as doves"* (Matthew 10:16).

The *student club* is a regular feature of American educational life. Typical are sports clubs, language clubs, debating societies and the like. For the young Christopher, however, certain particular clubs provide an excellent ground to sow the seeds of a democratic, God-fearing and God-loving way of life. In associations like a school newspaper or magazine, or a dramatic club, young people must inevitably concern themselves with ideas and ideals, with the spoken and written word. In addition, the public speaking class and the debating team furnish further opportunities to gather the know-how of presenting ideas clearly, concisely and convincingly.

Many of these clubs have taken on increasing importance because they affect the total character of *campus life* and *student movements* in general. Incidentally, the term "campus" means more than just the collegiate version. We refer as well to junior high school, high school, junior colleges and in some cases even business schools — in short, wherever students gather for extracurricular activities.

Leadership in student life is first established within the various clubs and a candidate for school office is often judged by his activity in smaller organizations. To the Christopher, who looks upon himself as a *lay missionary* among his classmates rather than a mere sponge absorbing facts, participation in these activities is of tremendous value because in them guidance can be offered, thought and action influenced — for *good!*

At all levels of education, we who possess the truth must have *clear aims, initiative, a sense of dedication* — for what is *good*. We must work unceasingly, learn the art of *plausibility* and devote ourselves to train, and be trained, to bring back Christ into our schools, into our classrooms, and into all phases of life.

The woman who went back to teaching after having left it earlier to go into business, the scientist who left his laboratory and took a cut in pay in order to bring "strong Christian values" into the teaching end of science, the secretary who became an assistant to the department head of a well-known university so she could get into the fight for good with the same determination that others were showing in battling for evil — these and thousands more like them have shown what can be done to "overcome evil by good."

True, they are only small beginnings. But once others begin to realize what they can do, individually and personally, in the field of education to save the world, this trend, God willing, shall begin to snowball into something of major proportions. Then shall personal considerations and conveniences slip back into being matters of secondary importance. The thrill of building instead of destroying, of spreading light instead of darkness, peace instead of confusion, love instead of hatred, will more than compensate for any sacrifices entailed.

Surely there must be — there are! — at least one million persons of all faiths in our country who are determined to further the common good of all. What inspiration they will impart to the millions of students who look for — and have a right to expect — the best training that the *best* Americans can and will give them!

But let us not forget for one moment that a change for the better will take place only when, as, and if those who know better — the good, God-fearing parents, teachers and even students — dedicate themselves to this Christ-like task. After all, it comes down to a matter of arithmetic. Only in proportion as the bearers of light go into the important field of education will the darkness disappear. If only a few go, then most of the darkness must remain.

Make no mistake about it. The fate of our country and of the world for a long time to come may depend on whether these one million Americans accept or reject the personal responsibility and privilege of showing interest in teaching the tens of millions in our schools the right things — about their lives, their country, and their world!

CHAPTER FIVE

Government

Your Job to Make It Good

"We must not be confused about the issue which con-
fronts the world today. That issue is as old as recorded
history. It is tyranny versus freedom. Tyranny has,
throughout history, assumed many disguises, and has
relied on many false philosophies to justify its attack
on human freedom. Communism masquerades as a
doctrine of progress. It is nothing of the kind. It is, on
the contrary, a movement of reaction. It denies that
man is master of his fate, and consequently denies man's
right to govern himself. And even worse, communism
denies the very existence of God. Religion is persecuted
because it stands for freedom under God. This threat
to our liberty and to our faith must be faced by each
one of us."   *Harry S. Truman*

In country after country all over the world the design for
godless conquest of all mankind follows its sinister pattern. In the
United States the subversives' success has been increasingly great,
due to the widespread indifference of so many otherwise good
people who often make the excuse that they want "no truck with

dirty politics," forgetting that politics, in its purest definition, is the *art* and *science* of government.

The results of a Gallup poll conducted recently showed that sixty-seven percent of American parents do not want their children to go into politics, one of the reasons being that the whole field of politics is bad. However, twenty-one percent of the parents held that unless people with good ideas *do* go into politics and into government, "democracy will die."

In the first group, it is painfully obvious, are those who do not participate actively in whatever pertains to the running of this country. They concern themselves very little with primary, state or national elections. They seldom run for office. Witness, for example, the Minnesota newspaper headline, "5 Decline to Run for Municipal Post," which captioned the story of five St. Paul attorneys who refused to be candidates for a municipal court judgeship.

Too often theirs is the characteristic American attitude toward government and even toward the subversive threat to undermine it. Americans are aware of the threat, at least dimly, yet they have done too little about it.

To Get Down to Cases

Generally speaking, when an individual in America thinks of himself in connection with government, his chief concern is with the question of whether or not he wishes to be a "politician." Actually, however, every one of you is deeply involved in and affected by the processes of government, whether you realize it or not. Every time you pay a sales tax, get a ticket for parking or speeding in your car, or fill out an income tax form, you are involved with the government. Every time you go before a labor board as an employer or as an employee, every time you collect unemployment insurance or old-age security benefits or workmen's compensation, you are involved with the government. Every time you see fire, police or sanitation departments in operation, you are watching government in action.

It is difficult, indeed, to think of any human activity in our modern society where the impact of government is not felt. Obviously, then, you need not be a politician to be concerned with the legislative, judicial and executive behavior of your nation.

Governments are instituted among men to secure the rights given to you by your Creator. Through governments you can place under popular control those institutions which will protect you against a willful, evilly purposeful minority and which will further your common aims and aspirations.

The greatest ills in many nations have arisen from the fact that people are not sufficiently interested in their government. Public apathy encourages official corruption. Failure to use the rights bestowed by democracy advances the rapid growth of dictatorship. If people as a whole withdraw from the arena of politics, then selfish and tyrannical minorities can and do monopolize the great powers of government.

To illustrate: suppose for a moment that our nation were a community of one hundred instead of the hundred million and more that we have. And suppose these one hundred people had no government at all. It would then be possible for half a dozen men of ill will, prototypes of our modern gangster, to arm themselves with brass knuckles, clubs and guns and to terrorize the entire community, to deny to the entire community the right to live as free people.

The power of the gangster to take over is not some mythical concept. It has happened in many American cities where organized gangs have joined with self-seeking politicians in running whole communities, looting the public treasury, disregarding the public interest for the benefit of the gang and its cronies in office.

In our lifetime, actually, gangs have taken over entire *nations.* Still fresh in peoples' minds is the example of the Nazis in Germany. The Hitler movement started with armed gangs, street ruffians who beat up people and broke up peaceful meetings. The shock troops and the storm troops and the gigantic open-air spectacles were an enlargement of that gang idea. Finally, the Nazis seized power and used government, not to secure the right of the German citizenry, but to *destroy* those God-given rights.

Still tragically fresh in our memory also is the way in which the Communists proceeded to "convert" once-democratic nations in eastern Europe into police states. They applied a blueprint for power used by the godless. And that blueprint can be applied to the United States, hastened along by the apathy of people with regard to their government. While the nation sleeps, the totalitarians bore their way into one post after another. When the opportune time comes, they reach out for *total* power.

There has been no dearth of diagnoses on the subject. However, the fact still remains that so far, too many experts have done more to define this *disease* in our modern society than they have taken steps to halt its freedom-sapping inroads.

In a nation such as ours, founded on the recognition of man's God-given rights and his *eternal* relationship to his Creator, founded more firmly on these basic truths than any other nation on the face of the earth, such apathy and indifference are inexcusable.

One main characteristic of the democracy which is our Republic is the belief in the inalienable rights of the individual. A second characteristic is the belief in the necessity for democratic control of political and economic life. These two articles of faith constitute the foundation of our democratic tradition.

We as a nation have our faults. But these faults are small indeed compared with the deliberate pattern of personal and public falsehood, political chicanery, and godless propaganda of the totalitarian.

Obviously anyone who shares these views has no place in our government, and must be weeded out. To make a comparison: if you want to get rid of weeds in a garden, *plant something* in their stead. If you want to get rid of darkness, bring in *light*. If you want to get rid of disease, initiate measures that will insure health.

If you want good government — and the overwhelming majority of Americans do want sound administration — then you must work to put in people with sincerely honest, truly American ideas, if you cannot go in yourselves.

The First Step

The first step in that direction is to become aware of our historical roots. Thus it is both startling and upsetting to realize that many people, particularly those of the younger generation, have grown up ignorant of the Christian heritage which is America's.

The proof?

Instruction concerning the Declaration of Independence (the main charter and guiding spirit of our governmental structure for eleven years, from 1776 to 1787, when the Constitution based on the principles of the Declaration was adopted and ratified) is required by law in only nine states. The conclusion to be drawn from this startling fact is contained in the words of Woodrow Wilson:

"No more vital truth was ever uttered than that freedom and free institutions cannot long be maintained by any people who do not understand the nature of their own government."

This being so, the time has certainly arrived for every God-fearing citizen in our land to take steps to see that this condition is corrected at once, to see that all our people, young and old, are thoroughly schooled in all that their democracy meant in the past and will mean to them in the future. As an American taxpayer, *you* have both the right and the obligation to *insist* on results. If you live in a state that does not demand explicit teaching on the Declaration of Independence, you can start the ball rolling to see that it, the Constitution, and the Bill of Rights become integral parts of the policy and teaching of *every* school, from kindergarten to university, to which you pay taxes or make gifts.

Don't be satisfied with mere teaching by rote. See that the spirit as well as the letter is imparted to students. Be concerned that all our young people should know the high price paid for liberty by our forefathers and be ready to pay the same price, if need be. "Never take your country for granted," said Alice Duer Miller, "because men have broken their hearts to get it for you."

If you are in one of the nine states that do require teaching of the Declaration, check to see *how* it is actually being taught. Check to see whether it is being side-tracked, ignored, or belittled. Leave nothing to chance! Don't be satisfied with an incidental reference to it in a government, history or civics course. Insist on its being required teaching. And make sure it is not being taught by someone who explains that it was a "good" statement — for the eighteenth century.

Persuade every organization to which you belong or with which you are acquainted to concentrate on the one objective of having these basic fundamentals taught and respected in all phases of local, state and national activity. This means more than lip service, more than hanging a copy of the Declaration on a wall, more than a colorless reference to the mere letter of these fundamental documents.

It means infusing the living spirit of the Declaration, the Constitution and the Bill of Rights into every segment of private and public life in the United States.

And remember also the inspiration of all these documents — the Creator of the world and of everything and everyone in it. To repeat again the words of William Penn: "Those people who are not governed by God will be ruled by tyrants."

Schooling for Government

While it is true that a nation, like a city, may never catch up with its dreams of the future, it is certain that proper guidance and training of fine young Americans for public service in government are the best guarantees against both corrupt and subversive inroads. They are the most positive assurance of good, honest democratic administration now and in the future.

In the early years of its history, America was able to draw on the best men in the country to serve the whole nation in positions of public trust. Washington, Jefferson, Franklin, Adams and many others came at the call of duty to any office the nation needed to fill. Since the end of the Civil War we have seen a growing disinclination on the part of our citizens to enter public service either for long or short periods, although millions of our young men and women have made and will make any sacrifice and give up any advantage to serve in the armed forces when our country is in danger from without.

Today our danger is also from within. And we need men and women who will serve without the stimulus of war, without public recognition, perhaps without public appreciation, in positions which are often as important to the survival of our nation as is service in the armed forces.

To go into government sometimes may mean, of course, a loss of some portion of your normal earning power. Yet such *a seeming disadvantage* is far outweighed by the many advantages you, individually, will receive. "In business, profit and loss are the criteria of success," Defense Secretary James Forrestal once commented. "In government, your rewards for successful work are much less tangible. They come from the inner satisfaction of taking part in the most important and powerful and complicated team in the world, and not from individual compensation."

Your Particular Niche in Government

Direct, personal participation in a specific position is, of course, the most constructive means of shaping the character of your government, as has been pointed out previously. Without dwelling further on this particular phase of your participation, there are two principles which it would be well to bear in mind.

One is that a public position, from the lowliest civil servant on up to the President of the United States, is a public trust. If there be corruption in high places, there will be cynicism in low places. People will begin to look upon *all* government as rotten, will learn to look upon democracy as an ugly farce, will lose faith in democratic leadership. For you, as a Christopher, to hold public office, whether as a tax collector or as a Congressman, means that you will have to devote yourself to strengthening the belief of the common man in the efficiency and honesty of free, democratic government. In short, put public welfare above personal gain. Don't go in to do *well* for yourself but to do *good* for others.

A second principle for a Christopher is to prove to the people that they can be free and still be *fed,* that great liberty and good living can go hand in hand. Failure to meet the economic needs of the people through an intelligent use of government can create a loss of faith just as surely as corruption in government destroys interest in our free way of life. Economic chaos creates political chaos, and out of political chaos arise dictatorships and world upheaval.

If, however, you cannot go into the field of government yourself, you can still be listed in either of two classifications: the *electorate* or the *loyalty group.*

The Electorate

By the electorate is meant all those who are eligible to vote. To be part of the electorate is to be the inheritor of a great tradition, a precious, God-given right achieved after long struggle and much suffering. But just as man tends to neglect other aspects of his inherited rights, so does he tend these days to neglect his right to vote. *He abuses the privilege by neglecting it.* Decades ago the great majority of those Americans who were eligible took part in presidential elections; in recent years the numbers have fallen off sharply.

Realize what this means. If only thirty percent of the population votes, then it is possible for a body of human beings composed of only fifteen percent of the total electorate to elect its spokesman to *govern* the nation. That means eighty-five percent of the electorate would be taking orders from fifteen percent of the people. Anyone could hardly blame this fifteen percent if it were finally to conclude that a dictatorship would be as acceptable as a democracy since seventy percent of the people don't care to exercise their democratic rights.

The consequence of this abstinence from the polls is far-reaching. In the past it has made it easy for political machines to be set up that were little interested in the public good. Secondly, totalitarian elements find it not too difficult to slip their standard bearers into public office when the great mass of electors stays home on election day. And these totalitarians make their task even easier by using democratic lingo and democratic processes to subvert and destroy democracy. In short, failure to use your ballot smooths the way for the corrupt politicians, for the selfish lawmakers, for the subversives to dominate the machinery of government *while they are still in the minority* — a condition which is quite contrary to the entire spirit of democracy where the majority decides public policy while still recognizing minority rights.

The Christopher, therefore, must be a voter. Too, he can get his family, friends and neighbors to vote. He can become a canvasser on election day to help turn out the vote for the principles in which he believes, can carry his citizenship with a sense of genuine responsibility, can become a living part of his community.

The Loyalty Group

The loyalty group is a regular part of our society, as intrinsic to the making of public policy as are the various local assemblies or even the Congress of the United States. Such groups are merely combinations of persons banded together to affect popular thought by joint action. Some groups are good; some are bad — depending on your point of view and the moral worth of the issues involved.

They exist for two reasons. First, when we elect a candidate to an office, we do so because of a general attitude concerning him or her — party affiliation, honesty, perhaps even good looks. And once the candidate is elected we seek openly to get him or her to favor some special piece of legislation which affects us deeply. Second, we may wish to educate or arouse the community on some issue so that there will be a constant pressure on all sections of society to swing into action.

Doing this takes many forms — letter writing and telegrams, meetings and parades, lobbyists and delegations, media publicity and general advertising. Almost everybody is a member of some such group. It may be a trade union or a taxpayers' league or any of a whole host of easily recognizable gatherings. Here again a special duty falls upon the shoulders of the Christopher: the duty of acting in any such group with *purpose* and with *intelligence*.

A Christopher should ask himself or herself three questions when aligning with a cause. First, *what* is its purpose? Second, *how* does it intend to realize its purpose? Third, *who* controls the group?

Purpose should be examined closely. Too many people fall for a phrase. Sometimes the phrase is good, like "we want peace." But often as not the supposed road to peace may be a road to war. A cliche is not a solution. The more dishonest a group is, the more cynically it will hunt for high-sounding phrases to catch the unwary.

How a group intends to realize its purpose is as vital a consideration as its aims. A foul means for an allegedly good end generally winds up as a foul end.

Who controls an organization is a matter which should be thoroughly investigated. Gullible citizens are too often tricked into joining a group, paying dues, lending a name to a letterhead, only to find out much later that the organization they support has become a loathsome thing in the hands of unscrupulous people who have *perverted* its original purpose. The real character of any group can only be determined by the character of those who are *in control.* Look particularly to see who is secretary of the organization to which you belong or which you intend to join. Check also on the editor of the group's official journal (if it has one), and investigate, also, those on the nominating committee who make the policy of the organization.

When these questions have been asked, and answered satisfactorily, the duty of the Christopher when he or she joins an organization is to participate *personally* in its activities. Go to meetings. Be alert. Know what goes on. Accept posts of responsibility. Vote in the elections. It is up to you, *individually,* to see that these pressure groups are utilized to *strengthen* your democracy, not to weaken it; that they are used to liberate each individual, not enslave him. Remember: to be a positive influence for good, you must be on the spot, meeting your fellow citizens and making your *living* presence felt.

These Lead the Way — You Can Follow

The best way to show what *can* be accomplished in the field is to demonstrate by actual cases what *is being done* right now by some of those who have made public service their life's work. The old saying of the skeptics, "I'm from Missouri; show me," can most effectively be answered by *living examples.* Consider, then, the following, typical of hundreds of cases like them:

One man, motivated by the desire to *serve* his country as others were trying to destroy it, ran for Congress and was elected not long ago. One of his recent talks, according to those who heard it, figuratively "pulled them out of their seats" with the soundness and enthusiasm of his presentation of vital American doctrines.

A young man from Michigan, very much interested in the labor-relations phase of government, gave up a position in a manufacturing plant to go into federal service where his zeal for good could be more widely felt.

A young woman in Boston went to Washington, secured a position on the staff of a senator, and now is personally responsible for many important documents of factual data on one of the Senate committees.

Four young people, three men and one woman, gave up business careers to join the staff of the United Nations organizations. Two are interpreters, one a secretary, another a clerk.

Another Christopher, a man in his late thirties, resigned as plant foreman to run for office in his local community. Though without previous political experience, the soundness of his platform and the honesty of his approach helped defeat a small, well-entrenched political machine. "When I started out, people told me I was crazy, that it couldn't be done," he said. "I was polite and listened to 'em… then I went ahead and did it!"

A college graduate, after serving in the Merchant Marine during the war, has enrolled for an intensive training course with the view to entering the U.S. Foreign Service.

A lawyer in California offered his services and was accepted by the state Senate Committee on Education for the purpose of analyzing textbooks.

All these cases and numerous others paralleling them are tremendous steps in the right direction. Yet they are but a comparative drop in the bucket when the *vastness* of the field is realized. The opportunities to get into this vital phase of our national life are almost limitless. *It is up to you* to see that these opportunities are not wasted. When instances like those cited are multiplied thousands of times over, then much of the foreboding about how our government and nation may be misled will be dispelled.

Some Practical Suggestions

To assist in this, here are a few tips which it might be well to follow:

1. Know and make your voice heard by your local municipal officials.
2. Know your congressional representatives and make your influence felt by them, too.
3. Follow newspaper reports on how your Congressman or Congresswoman votes on various pieces of legislation.
4. Keep abreast of the issues before your local, state and national governments.
5. Register and vote in primary, state and national elections.
6. Join civic groups (after proper investigations as to their purpose, methods and personnel) and be active in such groups.
7. Encourage others who can, to go *personally* into all phases of government work with the motive of *preserving* the God-given rights which subversives are trying to uproot from our free way of life.
8. Go yourselves — as *Christophers* — if it is humanly possible

and in the spirit of *"Be doers of the word, and not merely hearers"* (James 1:22).

Democracy's battle for existence is never finished.

In every classroom, in every government office, in every legislative and judicial chamber, the words of the Declaration of Independence should be publicly displayed and lived up to. And in every heart their meaning should guide every thought, word and action. With our Founding Fathers you can defend these God-given rights and with them you can echo the words:

"We hold these truths to be self-evident:

1. That all men are created equal;
2. That they are endowed by their Creator with certain inalienable rights;
3. That among these are life, liberty, and the pursuit of happiness;
4. That, to secure these rights, governments are instituted among men, deriving their just powers from the consent of the governed;
5. That, whenever any form of government becomes destructive of these ends, it is the right of the people to alter or to abolish it, and to institute a new government, laying its foundation on such principles, organizing its power in such form, as to them shall seem most likely to effect their safety and happiness."

Finally, to repeat the words the men who founded this Republic used in closing the Declaration of Independence:

"And for the support of this Declaration, with a firm reliance on the protection of divine Providence, we mutually pledge to each other our lives, our fortunes, and our sacred honor."

These men dared everything to win the God-given heritage which is yours today. You, as a Christopher, relying on the same Divine Guidance, can do no less than to work unceasingly to preserve this heritage for yourself and for posterity.

CHAPTER SIX

Labor-Management

Tremendous Issues at Stake

A short time ago in a large Midwestern city, I had occasion to visit a friend of mine, a vice president of a well-known manufacturing concern. He is a fine chap, what most people would refer to as a "nice guy," civic-minded, and a person anyone would be glad to know. However, in talking with him about the labor-management situation in general and the part of the individual worker in that situation in particular, he showed that he had a blind spot where his role in the business world was concerned. A "blind spot," incidentally, which you or I could easily have possessed had we been in his position, taken up as he was with the problem of running a very complicated industrial concern.

A long and costly strike had just recently been settled with his employees, and this executive, a ruddy-faced, extremely energetic man with a mind like the proverbial steel trap when it came to analytical figures and industrial problems, was anything but a cold, hard businessman when I saw him.

Pacing back and forth in his office for the better part of twenty minutes, he kept exploding about the ingratitude of people who were never satisfied with getting just treatment and fair wages.

"They always want more," he almost shouted. "Give 'em an inch and they'll take a yard. Give 'em decent working conditions, paid vacations, health benefits — everything — and what happens? They go on strike because they say we're 'unfair to labor'! I don't get it. It beats me!"

I asked him if he really wanted to know the cause of much of his company's trouble. A sudden stop in his pacing and an incredulous, "Now don't tell me *you* know!" was his only answer.

So, with this doubtful encouragement, I plunged in:

"Granting that you've done all you say you have," I told him, "you've still overlooked one very important item. You haven't given your employees *yourself.*"

At that, the roof almost fell in. "Given them myself? Are you crazy? What do you want me to do? Go around the plant and play nursemaid to workers who wouldn't appreciate it even if I were stupid enough to try it?"

"You miss the point," was my reply. "You don't have to be a nursemaid to anybody, but you do have to be a human being where your workers are concerned. To you, your employees are just so many cogs in a wheel. You don't really *know* them, and they don't know you. Don't fool yourself. People resent not being treated as *individuals.* There's dignity in every human being and every human being likes to be treated as one. If you and your associates got out and made it your business to take a *sincere,* friendly interest in those who work for you (and I do mean a *sincere interest,* because people have a sort of 'sixth sense' about things like that; they can tell what is genuine and what isn't) I guarantee relations between you and them would be a whole lot better."

"Friendly interest, ha!" The reply almost blasted my eardrums. "That's so much twaddle! This is a business we're running, not a Sunday school!"

He was still muttering, almost sorrowfully, under his breath about people who weren't businessmen sticking to the things they knew something about, when we left his office that Saturday afternoon and got into his car to drive out of the plant. As we reached the main gate, a company policeman started to wave us through when this vice president suddenly stopped the car and stuck his head out of the side window.

"Afternoon, Jim," he told the cop with a curt smile. "Have a good weekend!"

The look on the gateman's face was a picture no artist could have painted. From a sort of surly politeness, his expression changed to one of incredulous surprise, as much as to say, "What goes on here? He's never done this before." Then, quickly, he managed a grin and a "Thanks a lot, Mr. _____! Same to you!"

When we were safely out of earshot, this executive turned to me with the air of a man who has made a startling discovery. "Darned if it didn't work!" was his amazed comment, and you could almost see the little wheels in his brain telling him, "This is good business. Friendliness really pays off."

To him his discovery was encouraging and, in a limited sense, it was to me, too. Yet, withal, it only scratched the surface of what was the cause of his, and of most human, troubles. If his friendliness had sprung out of a genuine love of his fellowman, of that gateman and of all his other employees, it would have furnished a solid beginning in eliminating the friction between management and labor. It would have paved the way toward better social justice on both sides: fair wages and fair work, decent working conditions for employ*ees*; a decent respect for the rights of employ*ers*. This human recognition of the rights and duties of both capital and labor will prove, totalitarian propaganda notwithstanding, that the evils that afflict our human society *are not necessarily* inherent in our American economic system.

The solution is *not* to overturn our civilization as Communism would do, to take away property rights so man will no longer cheat and steal, to legalize the evil of class warfare and class hatred in order to arrive at the goal of a classless society.

The solution lies in the daily application of the Divine Law promulgated by Christ of Galilee. And this application will reform not only our morals, but our institutions as well.

Every man is created in the Image and Likeness of God and, in that, *we are our brothers' keepers*. We are what we would have others be to us!

People do want to have others take an interest in them. They don't want to be patronized. Sure, a man or a women has to earn a living and wants to be decently paid; but he and she want more than money. They want to be treated in such a way as to be able to maintain the independent dignity which is their right — which is just another way of saying they want to be loved.

And they, in turn, do want to be their brothers' keepers!

The Rights and Duties of Labor

On one hand, workers with a Christopher purpose should strive to carry out honestly and well all equitable agreements freely made, without violence, disorder or outrage upon employers. They should accept just wages and not agitate for an immoderately higher rate of pay, which might imperil the economic soundness of a concern and bring about hardships for both employer and workers.

The Christopher-minded employers, on the other hand, should treat workers as *free* people, as co-partners in ownership, profits and management, and thus avoid extremes of both the left and the right. Those not possessed of considerable wealth — in short, the workers — are more defenseless against poverty and injustice than employers, hence an employer should, to quote Pope Leo XIII's great encyclical, *Rerum Novarum:*

> "…never tax his work people beyond their strength, nor employ them in work unsuited to their sex or age. His

great and principal obligation is to give to everyone that which is just."

Thus, because management is in a more advantageous position, it has a greater obligation. In every country where it has failed to guard the security of the worker, it has prepared the way for its own destruction.

There is, however, *a double danger* to be avoided — as another encyclical, *Quadragesimo Anno,* issued by Pope Pius XI, pointed out. "On the one hand," to quote the encyclical, "if the social and public aspect of ownership be denied or minimized, the logical consequence is *Individualism,* as it is called: on the other hand, the rejection or diminution of its private and individual character necessarily leads to some form of *Collectivism.* To disregard these dangers would be to rush headlong into the quicksands of Modernism with its moral, juridical and social order, which We condemned in the Encyclical Letter issued at the beginning of Our Pontificate."

As remedies for the economic evils of the day, Leo proposed a return to the social and moral principles of Christianity and advocated *limited* intervention by the government as the guardian of public welfare and prosperity within the framework of justice. Workers were to be fairly paid, decently fed, clothed and housed. Harmful child labor was to be stopped, workers' health protected, justice assured in negotiations and contracts. Finally, Leo concluded in his encyclical, which has come to be recognized by people of all faiths as a "Christian Manifesto on Labor," the state must remove causes of industrial conflict and control outbreaks of strife.

Leo was far ahead of his time, since such ideas were almost heresy to the world of 1891. Since then, however, others have similarly concerned themselves with questions of social justice.

Thus, in the modern era, a pattern has been set forth by

people of all religions and adhered to even by those with no formal religion but who do have a good sense of moral values. This unanimity of opinion in such a vital field is significant for *another* reason in addition to that of a desire for social justice, however. It emphasizes the fact that religion *and* labor *are the two greatest bulwarks against totalitarianism in this country.*

Labor and Capital Need Each Other

By no means is it suggested now or ever that some of the evils in our economic life, about which totalitarians rant and rave, do not exist in our country. Sad to say, they do exist — but the elimination of these evils does not require the destruction of our economic system. Again, the fault lies not so much in the system as in the *greediness of man* himself. And, in attempting to resolve this condition, it must be realized very clearly that there will always be areas of difference between employers and employees. However, the Christopher point of view holds that these differences can exist without serious detriment to either side, *provided* honesty, decency, a sense of fair play and acknowledgment of man's God-given dignity, rights and responsibilities are *mutually* recognized.

In other words, both sides must *play the game according to the rules.*

So far in the United States, thank God, capital and labor have been allowed the opportunity of ironing out their varied differences *within the framework of our democracy.*

In many respects they have been able to draw more closely together through institutions and organizations which, on both sides, are able to present their points of view intelligently and, generally speaking, express the majority viewpoint of each group as a whole.

In the field of labor, undoubtedly the most important of these organizations is the union, operating on the biblical theory that *"Two are better than one, because they will get a good wage for their labor. If the one falls, the other will lift up his companion. But woe to the solitary man! For if he should fall, he has no one to lift him up."* (Ecclesiastes 4:9-10).

Unions and the labor field in general offer a tremendously fertile field of activity for the Christ-bearer — the Christopher — who is aware of the necessity of bringing truth and its attributes to bear for the social justice of all.

The men and women in these unions look to their leaders, great and small, for guidance in many spheres outside their own particular activity. The nature of that leadership, whether it be for better or worse, for *good* or for *evil*, depends on the part that every individual union member plays within his or her own group.

A Little Work Can Accomplish Wonders!

To give one striking example of the way in which Christian ideals can be put to work in the labor movement:

For the better part of a decade one powerful local branch of a newspaper union in the Eastern United States was the target — and a vulnerable target, at that — of intensive subversive activity because of the union's influence all over the country. There was an opposition group, too, but until recently it was largely ineffectual. The people in the latter group knew what they wanted, but lacked the necessary know-how. The missing links were: *organization, inspiration, and manpower.*

A couple of years ago, prodded by some good, hard-working unionists, this group began really to do something. Meeting monthly, it brushed up on trade union practices, social action philosophy, and parliamentary procedure. It acted as a sort of clinic to thrash out various important labor problems and so became conversant with the entire labor picture in that particular locality. It studied the tactics of those who were entrenched in power, among them the contact methods that they had exploited to the best possible advantage. It got as many union members on the various committees as it could, in order to silence the administration's claim that the opposition did much talking but little union work.

Motivated by a sincere Christian love of their fellow men and women, they copied the subversives' tactics of interesting themselves in *every* union member, especially those who were uncertain or on the fence as regards being morally right or subversively wrong.

Not long ago, the development of this approach won a complete victory. The scales swung decisively in favor of the sound, God-fearing majority which, for too long, had been unable or too apathetic to make its wishes heard. But the crux of the whole victory for the forces of light was *activity.* The actions of the well-informed, intelligent rank-and-file members helped mold the future of the union. And, of course, self-sacrifice in attending union and committee meetings helped too. It was a tough battle, but it brought results.

In practice these unionists put into action the principles for good economic living. The application of these same principles, as applied to the whole labor-management field, has been summed up very concisely in the *"Code for Industrial Peace"* published by the Institute of Industrial Relations of East St. Louis and Belleville, Illinois. Quoting briefly from this code:

"We acknowledge the Brotherhood of Man under the Fatherhood of God. Hence we recognize in every man or woman, whether manager or laborer, the dignity, the sanctity and the eternal destiny of the human person. We further recognize that people as human beings and as members of civil society have certain inalienable rights, which no one, however powerful, can violate without injustice.

"Management and Labor both perform essential functions in society, the one complementing the other in the production and distribution of commodities and services necessary and useful for human living. They are interdependent units of the same organic whole; therefore, what is good for one is good for the other, and what hurts one hurts the other.

"Management and Labor have the solemn duty of mutual cooperation towards achieving an economic structure in which each individual will be enabled to fulfill his obligations of Social Justice, that is, of making his proportionate contribution to the general welfare.

"The sincere application of justice, good faith, and fair dealing ... is the indispensable means of securing an equitable working out of the natural rights of man embodied in the Declaration of Independence and the Bill of Rights. Only thus can America's future as a free nation be assured."

It is up to the Christopher — the Christ-bearer — to bring this glorious concept of the dignity of both the worker and the employer back into our economic life. A comparative few, working in the spirit of Truth, can bring sanity and decency back into this vital phase of our national life — where these virtues rightfully belong!

In doing this, they will be one with the Carpenter of Nazareth, Who Himself knew what it was to toil and labor. In doing this, they will literally be helping to carry Christ into the marketplaces of our country — and eventually into the whole world.

CHAPTER SEVEN

Writing

The Power of Words

Before anything in the world is ever done, *thought* precedes the *act*. From the time Gutenberg first invented the printing press and in increasingly higher proportion ever since, thoughts have nearly always been inspired by what someone put down in writing.

Centuries ago the chief means of spreading a thought, an idea, was by word of mouth, from a merchant to a customer, from a soldier to his family, from a trader in the market place to those grouped around to haggle over the quality of a piece of rare silk or a cannister of precious oil.

But what a contrast today! In the newspaper field alone, the daily pronouncements out of Washington, London, Paris, Rome or Moscow reach the ends of the earth within the space of a comparatively few minutes. Such has been the magic of modern science in multiplying the power of the wondrous *word*.

Words can be a power for *good* — or they can be a power for *evil*.

No more striking example of the truth of the second part of that statement can be found than the fate of Germany in the years immediately following the end of the First World War, when it began to forsake its struggle for democracy and to turn to the blandishments of Adolf Hitler. Right there the world witnessed one of the most terrifying demonstrations of the power of propaganda.

In newspapers, magazines, books, pamphlets, over the air, and in motion pictures, the German people were swayed, cajoled, perverted, hardened into an evil pattern of global conquest. Force of arms followed later, but ideas preceded the first *putsch*, the first territorial annexation, the first shot of World War II.

Today the virus of materialism, of totalitarianism, of perversion of all types is literally being forced upon us here in the United States — forced into our lives, our thoughts, our businesses, our homes, our families. And, to an astonishing degree, it has met with a favorable reception by those in our midst who are not basically bad but only gullible and unthinking.

Those behind this drive, those doers of evil, have a purpose, a goal. All their efforts are directed toward it. All their energies spent in the cause are just so many paving stones in the road to the conquest of light by those who live in the darkness.

That we have similar means at our disposal to fight for what is right is our hope, however. Yet it is a hope we must still fulfill, for up to now our efforts have been meager in comparison with those who would destroy our way of life, our freedom, our very civilization.

The Writing Field in America

Conveying ideas is one of the biggest industries in America today. We are influenced by the books, magazines, newspapers and advertisements we read, by the sounds that come over television and the radio, from scripts written in advance; by stage plays and by motion pictures.

All of these leave their imprint on us as individuals. They

help influence our thoughts, mold our tastes, determine our judgments, control our actions.

In broadcasting there have been outstanding examples of magnificent entertainment — splendid dramas, grand variety shows, brilliant musical presentations — which reflect the American public's innate good taste.

In many magazines and newspapers, in instances too numerous to mention, good writing and good, honest news coverage have helped to keep these two phases of the writing field relatively free and unfettered and a credit to our literary discrimination.

But in the motion picture industry, on the air, in the book world, in magazines and in newspapers, too much that is cheap and tawdry, too much that is immoral, too much that is materialistic and profane, have caused a lowering of literary standards at a rate that is truly alarming.

We do not expect all "cream" in our entertainment, but we do expect that the "milk" will not turn sour.

Most of us, for example, do not object to an occasional story about crime. We are not prudes. We are healthy-minded and decent. But we do resent a continuous and deliberate appeal to our baser instincts.

We resent in current literature, on the screen, over television and radio, all that is not merely subversive or obnoxious but actually dreary, repetitious, and decidedly unentertaining, because the writers are appealing not to most of the people, but to the few who prefer depravity and perversion. Yet while they may be appealing to a few, the effect on the general public is so far-reaching as to amount to a national tragedy.

Something to Do About It

There is some value, of course, in refusing to buy offensive or indecent literature, in turning off vulgar, boring or subversive radio and TV programs, and in abstaining from cheap movies. But the cure does not lie there, for it is like objecting to bad food without providing anything better. Good cooks must replace the bad ones, and in this case the cooks are the *writers*. They are the people who directly or indirectly prepare movie or television scripts, the news reporters who "talk" to millions, the authors of stories and articles, the novelists, the biographers, the playwrights.

And new and better writers can be found.

They will come from among *you*, the people of substance, of sound, healthy values — the vast group of Americans who constitute the backbone of our nation and of our Christian civilization. From among the tens of millions of you who are decent, honorable and law-abiding. You who have your feet on the ground, who are thoughtful and generous, genuine and stimulating. You Americans of every race and color can make a substantial contribution to the well-being of our country if, fortified with truth, you will go in large numbers into the writing field. It is one of the main fields in which the Christopher can work to change the world, to bring back integrity instead of untruth, individual responsibility instead of mass hypnotism, thought instead of mere sensationalism.

Words are the coinage of the world of ideas. It is even more important that words be honest than that money be honest. As the mind of the Christopher centers itself on Truth, his words will take on the simplicity and clarity of his purpose. He will be an island in which words that are clear and honest shine like a beacon through the prevailing fog of doubt and illusion.

In our world of mass communication, professional writing is one of the most important links joining people to people, or skillfully separating them (as do the godless) by planting doubt and hate. In the field of professional writing the Christ-bearer can find a wide scope for his or her work, provided, of course, that he or she has the talent for it. And that talent, incidentally, is much more generously distributed than most people realize.

We of the Christopher movement know from experience that this is so and it is of no use to protest, as some few do, "Perhaps you're right, but they still don't want worthwhile people in the writing field."

That is neither fair nor accurate.

Many with godless leanings have succeeded in infiltrating the writing sphere, of course, and have secured editorial and executive positions. But in contrast to these there is fortunately a far greater number of sound, sensible Americans who still hold similar posts. And these men and women definitely do want *good* material to be submitted for publication. Multiply their number, particularly of those who are articulate in supporting their beliefs, and the whole trend toward materialism in this field can not only be stopped but changed for the *better.*

One magazine editor recently remarked, "In my opinion, it is the failure to realize the message of interest and value they have for the modern world that keeps the majority of potential writers away from successful writing."

So the opportunity and the need for new writers with good ideas are there. Apart from the numerous possibilities in screen and broadcast writing, in the publishing end of the field alone there is scope enough for everyone with sufficient talent and perseverance to make a place for himself or herself.

Certain Laws of Writing

We do not claim that a person of substance and integrity can sell stories to magazines after ten easy lessons. Let's make that clear. There are certain laws of writing. The fundamental principles may be learned with comparative ease, but each branch of literature has its own special rules. "It takes years," said one of the nation's top writers, "to learn the wisdom, to acquire the experience that a writer must have. As far as the *craft* goes, you never learn it. Each piece of writing presents its own original problem of craftsmanship. Not every violinist can be a Heifetz or a Kreisler, but there are plenty of places for musicians outside the concert stage. Most of us want to start out as vice-presidents, when we should be content to begin as office assistants."

There is room for thousands of good writers. Out of these thousands, it is certain that a few will rise to the top of their professions, as cream rises to the top of milk. But famous-to-be or not, everyone counts. Some of you will find your particular talents better suited to one type of writing than another. Some of you will like to work only with facts, others with fiction. But for one who has a purpose, *a good* purpose — in short, a Christopher — the writing field offers a tremendous opportunity to spread *light* where there is *darkness,* to furnish entertainment as refreshing as it is wholesome.

Have a Purpose

To repeat: if you want to be a writer, the opportunities are there. But if you want to be a writer of *substance*, you must be inspired by higher ideals than merely making a living. The writer whose only object is dollars will turn out trite, lifeless material. While money is necessary, you will need a more dynamic motive if you are to survive the long, slow, often painful process which leads to success.

A far more vitalizing reward must inflame you with the ardor to keep on even in the face of difficult obstacles — the knowledge that you will be serving your fellow men and women. Like a doctor whose chief objective is to relieve suffering through the experience he or she has gained, the worthwhile writer is eager to share with others the ideals which dominate his own life as well as to interest and entertain. As one great editor says:

"Writers come from persons who have a story to tell or who are imbued with a desire to cause others to think as they think."

If you have a purpose, therefore, you have strength.

Set your standards high; you will find deep satisfaction in work well done.

You will be thrilled to explore and master new techniques, and possibly to start new trends in the craft of writing. As a Christopher writer you can bring the basic principles of Christ into literature with the same zeal, the same skill, the same perseverance which His enemies use to exclude Him. And because you are a Christopher, you can interpret human existence more faithfully.

You will have the satisfaction of knowing that the world is better because you have lived, have been useful, have played a part in renewing the face of the earth. *A writer who has the lofty desire to serve the common good inevitably rises above that frustration characteristic of those whose purpose is only their own private good.*

Writing can become a labor of love, a living prayer, a work which will ennoble and sanctify both you and all who read what you have written. You will be more interested in giving than in getting. You will think less of "taking out" of the world than of "putting in." *Hope* will carry you high over the disappointments, the rejections, the heart-wrenching failures which even the finest writers must suffer at first. You will know the deep and lasting joy of creative work; and you will play a real part in bringing to fellow men and women some of the true, the good and the beautiful that the Creator of all intended for all.

Writing Is Work

Good literature does not consist of 2,500 words dashed off in two hours. It takes time to write well. To become proficient in any art requires long practice.

But if you use the self-discipline which most successful writers find indispensable — that is, if you force yourself to write a certain minimum each day — you will make progress.

And just as important as writing is reading. A famous writer once said a good author reads six hours for every hour he writes. Read first-class literature, both the time-tested classics and the best work of modern authors. Read attentively; absorb the spirit and the tone of good writing. Learn its structures and techniques.

In the words of one editor: "There are a lot of people in the world who can write but lack the courage to keep at it, and there are a lot of people who have the courage but can't write. When you have the two together, the ability to write and the courage to keep at it, nothing in this world can stop you from succeeding."

Write for Everybody

Most beginners write to please themselves, not others. This can be a serious handicap. Try to key your stories to a mass audience, to the *many*, not merely the *few*, since the foundation of writers is actually twofold: (a) having something to say, and (b) having acquired through much practice the ability of saying what is to be said, to say it in a way that can be understood by most readers.

This can be done without compromising the content of your piece, for it is primarily a technique. The great exponent of the art of appealing to all was Christ Himself. He had the common touch. Normally, He spoke in words which all the people understood. Those who imitate Him in style as well as in content are well on the way to success. For example, many books have been written on Bernadette of Lourdes, but scarcely one had a circulation of more than a few thousand because all were "slanted" for five or ten percent of the faithful. Then a Jew, Franz Werfel, saw in Lourdes a tremendous story. He keyed his presentation to everyone, not just to a few. As a result, *The Song of Bernadette* has moved millions. And though Werfel had exceptional talents, at least in one respect you can equal him — that is, in writing for *everybody*.

Deepen Your Sense of Values

Contemporary literature is often unsubstantial, artificial, hard-boiled and cold-blooded. It deals with petty people and petty problems. And it emerges as petty writing simply because too many writers, having neglected to develop their spiritual nature, are destitute of strong values.

To achieve magnitude in your stories, you must first deepen and strengthen your own sense of values. A writer must *be* something. A great heart and an understanding mind can be developed through daily reflection or meditation, prayer, intimacy with the New and Old Testaments (from which the greatest writers have drawn much of their inspiration).

Even fiction should communicate an idea, a philosophy. Although the author's purpose is not to teach but to tell a story, into that story he inevitably will put what he believes, what he is. He must see reality *whole*, instead of ignoring great fundamental actualities, instead of concentrating on the superficial and accidental. Among those misleading the world are writers who believe and affirm that life ends with death, that the flesh is to be served blindly, that one's own gratification is the highest law of life.

Strive to Integrate the Human With the Divine

As a Christopher writer of fiction, you can do something few others are doing consistently today: not merely can you tell people how life should be lived — you can show what life really is. Like the manufacturer's book of specifications and directions found in the glove compartment of a new car, you can show the Creator's rules which are necessary for a whole and complete existence.

You must know the basic laws of human life before you can authentically depict character, the reaction of character to situation (source of dramatic conflict), and the enrichment or impoverishment of character wrought by dramatic conflict.

You must show through *action* how happiness or misery inexorably results from certain modes of action, how particular characters motivate specific kinds of action which change their lives and the lives of others for better or for worse. Truly realistic writing, in which the protagonists themselves push the action forward, is characteristic of great novels and stories.

Novelist Evelyn Waugh once wrote: "I believe you can only leave God out by making your characters pure abstractions. So in my future books there will be a preoccupation with style and the attempt to represent man more fully, which, to me, means only one thing, man in his relation to God."

If you agree that writing should be deeply significant but still doubt whether editors will buy such work, listen to what one of the most eminent editors in the country has told us:

"What makes quality in a piece of writing? The thing that makes pieces of writing dry as dust is lack of faith. Whenever a thing with faith, written with talent, is printed the public will buy it. Excellence in writing comes from a reaffirmation of universal truth. The reason there is hope for the Christian writer is that he has faith, the element that is missing in other writers."

But, he warned, this does not mean you should simply write *about* religious subjects. "Many writers write about religious themes, but with merely the intellectual approach. They give the impression perhaps that these things do not really mean much to them. That kind of writing does not attract readership. You must write *with* faith, a spirit of faith, not merely *about* faith, and then your writing will be avidly read."

Learn to Like People

The more you move among people, the more inspiration, warmth and compassion will characterize whatever you write. You will be convinced of at least the potential dignity of every person, of a lingering nobility in even the so-called dregs of humanity. You will know that every individual, no matter how mean or hateful, remembers real love and craves it from others.

If you have a consuming love for *all* men and women and not for just a *few*, if you are writing for *everyone* and not for just *some*, your writing will have warmth, friendliness and humanness which will appeal to all. Each time you find yourself stretching to the measure of Christ's sympathy and affection for all, you, too, will glimpse God's image in every person you meet — and reveal that insight in the things you write.

Follow Through

Expect difficulties. Booth Tarkington wrote for years before attaining recognition. Jack London had to sandwich his writing in between income-earning hitches at sea. Many a contemporary big time novelist or Hollywood writer began by slaving at half a cent a word. The few writers who have had big success on the first try are the exceptions.

A doctor doesn't attain skill and reputation in a year or two. He or she must go through college, medical school and internship. Avoid extremes of optimism or pessimism. Most beginners make the mistake either of underestimating their own buried talent or of expecting to write a bestseller or Hollywood smash hit the first crack out of the box.

Finally, perhaps you are not an exceptional writer. You may never be at the top of the list. But if you can write at all, you can be one of the *millions* of newspaper, book, magazine, radio, television and movie rank-and-file writers who, besides earning fair incomes, influence the thoughts of others.

If you can't take up writing on a full-time basis, write as a sideline. No matter what your work, you may be able to turn out something the public is hungry for. This would be doing your part in bringing Christian principles and ideals into the marketplace. And it would mean a little extra income, too.

Profit by rejections; they show the detours to be avoided. *But,* don't take them too seriously. Editor A may reject a manuscript which editor B snaps up with enthusiasm. And always — always — keep writing.

Remember — quitters never win. Winners never quit!

Writers should cherish that motto. Christopher writers should make it their special slogan in carrying Christ's truth not to just a *few,* but to *everybody!*

CHAPTER EIGHT

Personal Power and Social Responsibility

A few months ago while hurrying to keep an appointment in New York, I noticed, vaguely at first and then more consciously, that a small crowd had gathered in front of a shop on Park Avenue near 54th Street. Curiosity prompted me to stop and see what had caused such a show of interest. Peering over the heads of the crowd I saw, attractively framed and exhibited in large, bold-faced type, of all things, *a prayer* — a prayer that could be more than 700 years old! Its presumed author? St. Francis of Assisi. Pleasantly surprised at the setting, I read through those exquisite lines that flowed like some long-forgotten litany:

> Lord, make me an instrument of Thy Peace!
> Where there is hatred, let me sow love.
> Where there is injury, pardon.
> Where there is doubt, faith.
> Where there is despair, hope.
> Where there is sadness, joy!
> O Divine Master, grant that I may not so much seek
> To be consoled as to console,
> To be understood as to understand,
> To be loved as to love, for
> It is in giving that we receive,

It is in pardoning that we are pardoned,
It is in dying that we are born to eternal life.

Why those lines were put into that shop window I never found out. Yet because of the setting, the words seemed to radiate a special warmth and meaning. That simple prayer attributed to the Little Man of Assisi sums up freshly and perfectly the great need of our day: that each of us acknowledges his individual power as an "instrument" of peace; that each of us show individual initiative and assume personal responsibility in restoring to the world the love and the peace of Christ.

No matter who you are or what you are or where you may be, you can do something to change the world for the better. You count!

One of the most poignant yet dramatic illustrations of that belief in action is contained in the story of Ah Chai, an eight-year-old girl in South China who had leprosy. Hungry, alone, and wasted away with the disease which gnawed at her young flesh and bones, Ah Chai's life reached its supreme tragedy, so she thought, one hot summer's day when she was driven out of the village that had been her home by the villagers who hoped thereby to rid themselves of her pollution. So heartless and cruel was the fury of the mob which, armed with sticks and stones, shoved and pummeled her, that leprosy seemed fated to be cheated of its victory. And then it happened.

A missioner approaching the village from the opposite direction saw the commotion and quickened his pace until it became a trot and then his trot a run. Into the center of the crowd he went. A glance told him the child's condition, yet he didn't stop. Bending down, he picked up Ah Chai in his arms while the crowd fell back, shouting in warning: "Unclean … unclean!"

Cradled in the missioner's arm, the child stopped crying, but only for a moment. Then the torrent of tears began anew, yet this time they were tears of happiness, tears of gratitude that some-one cared.

"Why … why do you bother about me?" she asked between sobs. The priest swallowed hard and answered:

"Because God made you, just as He made me." And he continued, "That makes you my sister and makes me your brother. I'm going to take care of you. You'll never be hungry or homeless again."

"But how can I pay…?" Ah Chai started to ask, but the missioner smilingly shook his head for silence.

"All you have to do — all God wants you to do — is to return His love by showing that love to as many others as you can. Promise?"

A nod of a tear-streaked face was the eloquent reply.

That was when Ah Chai was eight. She died three years later, not long after her eleventh birthday. But in those three years she did much to bring the Love of God and His Peace into the lives of all the other lepers with whom she had to live and who were given to the missioners' care. She sang to them, she dressed their sores, she fed them, but most of all, she loved them.

When she died they expressed their gratitude, and thousands of other Chinese from the surrounding countryside echoed their feeling in these simple words: "Our little bit of Heaven has gone back to Heaven." And they would point upwards.

Even the "Least" Can Affect Thousands

If Ah Chai's story ended there, it would be inspiring enough. But it didn't. She is still doing good. Her life and what she did has been spoken about, told and retold, in countries all over the globe. Hearing it, people are deeply touched, yet the effect on them is invariably more than that. It gives them courage and hope. Once she realized her divine worth, this "least" of God's children was important, after all. She did count on earth ... for eternity.

And just as she thought with the vision of Christ, in terms of herself and of the world, so you can do likewise and your power for good becomes more effective and far-reaching. Once a person gains even a partial comprehension of the role he or she can play, personally and individually, everything takes on a new and hopeful aspect. The account of the three laborers who were working on a cathedral illustrates this.

The first man was a colorless-looking individual. When asked to define his job, his bored reply was that he spent all his time in cutting blocks of stone. And he added, "If I didn't have to earn a living for myself and family, I'd quit in a minute!"

The second man's job was to cut the timber that went into the building's construction. He, too, went about his work in a listless way, and in his continual complaining there was proof aplenty that his heart was not in his work.

The third laborer possessed none of the manual skill of the other two. He merely carried the stone and wood the others prepared. But he sang and whistled as he trudged back and forth with his heavy loads. To all appearances his work was the least attractive, the most monotonous and uninspiring, yet he went about it with zest and spirit. None of his fellow workers could understand it, and one day a newcomer who didn't know him very well asked him, point blank, the reason for his good humor. "What kind of work do you do?" was the way he put it. "What is your job?"

The cheerful laborer's reply was short and simple, yet it stressed the true perspective of all his toil. "What do I do?" he repeated. "Why, I'm building a cathedral!"

In a very real sense he *was* building a cathedral. While his role in the whole project was menial and insignificant, still he was a vital factor just the same. The structure couldn't rise without him — or someone like him. And because he had a big perspective, that perspective gave a big meaning to his little job.

In the same way, no matter how insignificant you may be or feel, you can still do something to change the world for the better. For those who try to be other Christs, there comes an understanding, experienced perhaps for the first time, of that real zest of living that God intended for all who are intent on using the talents entrusted to them for His glory and the good of others. Even if they possess only one talent, they do not bury it like the servant in the Scriptures who told his master, *"I was afraid, and I went and hid your talent in the ground. Here you have what is yours."* That man received the stinging and justified rebuke, *"You wicked and lazy servant"* (Matthew 25:25, 26), for his failure to put that talent to good effect. Ordering his other servants to take away that which had been freely entrusted to him, the master then concluded, *"For to all those who have, more will be given, and they will have an abundance; but from those who have nothing, even what they have will be taken away"* (Matthew 25:29).

For those with the ambition really to do good, ringing constantly in their ears is the challenge of urgency so well expressed in the words: *"I shall pass through this world but once. Any good, therefore, that I can do, or any kindness that I can show to any fellow creature, let me do it now. Let me not defer it or neglect it, for I shall not pass this way again."*

Not for a moment should a Christopher forget he has his own destiny to work out here and hereafter. Yet neither should he ever lose sight of the fact that he has a like obligation toward others. There is specific definiteness on this point in the command of Christ. While He said, *"You shall love your neighbor,"* He was very careful to give the measure of how much that love should be. *"As yourself,"* He said. There is no contesting that.

One of Christ's own apostles, St. James, seems to be even more emphatic on this point. *"Religion that is pure and undefiled before God, the Father,"* he says, *"is this: to care for orphans and widows in their distress, and to keep oneself unstained by the world"* (James 1:27). Note the emphasis he put on solicitude for others. Even if a person with weak faith starts to share with others the Truth he possesses, his own strength is thereby increased. He is like a run-down person who begins to exercise: the more he does it, the stronger he becomes.

Despite Misgivings

This opportunity — unfortunately, in some cases, the failure to realize such an opportunity exists — calls to mind an instance of a young man just out of the army after the close of World War II. He'd heard of the Christophers, so he informed us, and he came to us with this question: Did we think it worthwhile for him to take up work in one of the vital fields into which we are trying to direct a million Christophers in order to bring the world back to Christ and thereby insure peace?

The mere fact that he was undecided as to his future potential for good stressed the plight of so many people with fine ideas who underestimate their individual power to help return the world to Christ. Without putting it into words, this young man was saying, in effect, "Everything you say is okay, but what can a guy like myself do to push those ideas along? These days the ordinary person hasn't got a chance!"

It was explained to him, and he had the common sense to appreciate the truth of what was said, that peace is achieved not through government decree, but through the conscious, personal striving of the individuals who make up society. When it was pointed out that the great source of strength of one who works as a Christopher is the fact that he does not work alone, that Christ works with him and through him, a look of reassurance came over the young man's face. At the final words, "It comes down to this, Tom. God works through you — isn't that something?" With an amazed shake of his head he replied, "Gee, that *is* something, all right!"

That he was convinced God can and does work through ordinary mortals like himself, despite human limitations and weaknesses, is evidenced by the fact of his applying, and being accepted, for a post in the federal government where his influence for good, expressed in his enthusiastic adherence to sound, fundamental, God-given American principles has been a source of inspiration to all those around him. Literally, he is putting into daily practice the meaning of the words: *"For this was I born and for this I came into the world, to testify to the truth"* (John 18:37).

An Important Distinction

There are many basic reasons justifying consistent and continued emphasis on individual responsibility and participation in shaping the destiny of mankind.

First of all, the teeming millions of humanity are nothing more than you — one person — multiplied over and over again.

While it is almost impossible to overstress individual responsibility, it must still be pointed out that one extreme should be avoided. It is the exaggeration of the "individuality" of the individual to such an extent that the social nature of man is lost sight of and the dangers of "rugged individualism" allowed to step in and cause considerable harm. Each human being, while coming into the world as an individual, is likewise born a social being as a member of his *own* family and of the *whole human* family. That person must live as an individual, true, but also has obligations as the social being God intended. When rendering an account of his stewardship after death, there is a social as well as an individual consideration. For each of us there will be a particular judgment at which everyone is judged individually as to his own personal life. Then follows the general judgment in which all participate as members of the human race.

Therefore, while you can exert power for good, individually

and personally, you must ever be mindful that it should be exercised in terms of society and not in any isolated, anti-social sense. *"We are,"* as St. Paul reminds us, *"members of one another"* (Romans 12:5). And again, *"We do not live for ourselves, and we do not die for ourselves"* (Romans 14:7).

To Bear Fruit

Insofar as a person fulfills this role, he or she enjoys peace and happiness both here and hereafter. Yet constantly before one's mind's eye should be the eloquent reminder contained in the Scriptural parable of Christ and the fig tree. While beautiful in appearance and pleasing to the sight, Christ cursed it and it withered away. Why? The answer lies not in the fact that it was doing any harm, but only that it was doing no good. It produced only foliage, not fruit. And the latter was the purpose for which it was created: *"Early in the morning, as He was returning to the city, He was hungry. He noticed a fig tree by the road and so He went over to it, but He found nothing on it but leaves, and He said to it, 'May no fruit ever come from you again, forever!' And immediately the fig tree shriveled up"* (Matthew 21:19).

Individual Effort With Social Effects

There is no special "product" that you have to manufacture. Goodness is within each and every one, and all one has to do truly to bear Christ is to be a messenger, a distributor of that God-given attribute. Countless people all over the country, and indeed all over the world, have come to realize this.

Nothing is as convincing proof of the success of that "distribution of goodness" as are actual examples of people who have become Christ-bearers in their daily lives. One man, who as an individual feels a sense of responsibility to society and is doing something about it, wrote us as follows:

"Many times I have heard how fortunate it would be if enough persons with Christopher ideals would enter the teaching profession. I have finally decided to do that very thing and am going into the government and international relations field at the graduate level. I can see the importance of bringing the right values into the fields of government, politics, history and labor. Perhaps as a teacher I can help others see this necessity also. I am resigning a position in business that pays quite well, but feel so strongly about the crisis in which the whole world is becoming so deeply involved that I cannot have peace of mind if I do not do all in my power to help.... I'm 34 and have a family to care for, but God will bless our little attempt and all will come out well, I know."

In Boston one woman started a now-recognizable trend toward bringing the Christ Child back into Christmas greeting cards. Year in and year out she had listened to people complaining that most Christmas cards were too pagan. Determined to do all in her power to bring a religious note into the greetings being prepared for the birthday of Our Savior, she got a job with one of the largest greeting card companies for that very purpose. From the start she met with cooperation on all sides and, since this one pioneer Christopher sparked this trend, it has grown and is still growing. Her resourcefulness as an individual is certainly acting as a leavening force in our society.

Individuals Lead the Way

A student at Wellesley College, who confessed in the beginning that she belonged to "no church," heard a Christopher talk and found something in it which was to influence her life. The speaker's *"You count!"* stuck in her mind and stayed there even after graduation. She came to New York and got a job, not a very important one, in a radio station. Because of the knowledge that she, individually, mattered, all her better instincts soon rebelled at the actions of two editors who blue-penciled references in scripts to God and American ideals.

At first she tried, on her own, to get the deleted references back into the scripts. However, when the subversive activity increased, she went to the head of the department and respectfully suggested she thought it good business to keep the mention of God and democracy in the scripts instead of taking them out.

The department head, unaware of what had been going on, agreed. More than that, he personally made it his business to check the scripts for any blue-penciling from then on.

On a widely circulated magazine read by millions, another young woman has done, and is doing, equally effective work. She makes it her business to attend every union meeting of her craft and sometimes she is the only non-leftist present. "I feel like I'm in a room with 65 horse thieves," is the way she puts it. "But one little person like myself can accomplish something just by being there. They feel uncomfortable having someone present who knows they are horse thieves!"

Proof that Christopher action is not confined to the United States alone, but is worldwide, is found in the example of a woman-Christopher in South America. She made her field of Christ-bearing that of her national government, particularly the effort being made to pass a law erasing all reference to God from her country's schools. Personally undertaking a campaign of visiting every one of the one hundred and twenty-five legislators in the government, her reception was usually anything but pleasant. She was snubbed, ridiculed, given the runaround from one official to another. She was threatened with violence and several times even physically ejected by those who wanted no part of a bearer of Christ and who hated the very mention of His Name.

But still she kept on until they finally consented to see her. When the final vote was taken some weeks later, sixty-three voted to keep the idea of God in the schools while sixty-two were opposed. *One* vote made all the difference. And one woman who suffered more than a little was personally responsible for a victory that touched the lives of every person in her country.

You, whose light may have been temporarily dimmed by what the world has to offer in all that is material, can take heart and hope from the story of St. Francis Xavier. At the University of Paris, Xavier was very much the young sophisticate. He loved the things of this world and was little interested in those of the next. The warning of *"What good would it do a man to gain the whole world, but lose his own soul?"* (Matthew 16:26) was not unknown to him. But for too long he saw its meaning, if at all, as only *"through a glass, darkly"* (1 Corinthians 13:12).

And then one day, in a brief, suspenseful moment of self-examination, he finally caught the overwhelming significance of the words. If he, one individual, was worth so much, so then was *everyone.* He was consumed with a burning desire to share that knowledge with all mankind. He felt he had to get that idea across somehow to people wherever and whenever he could. How much of his life remained to him to complete this task he naturally didn't know. But it really didn't matter. Whatever he could do, he would do, to bring the knowledge of Christ to all. In ten years — the sands in the hourglass of his life ran out at forty-five — he reached, personally, nearly a million men, women and children.

One Small Voice

You who may feel you do not "know enough" to be of use as effective Christophers, remember — one small voice which makes itself heard on the side of the truth is often like a clarion call to action to those who can do something. A man out in the Midwest not long ago was chosen as a delegate to a widely publicized labor convention. The appointment, instead of flattering him, flustered him, especially in the face of some advice as to his responsibility in watching out for the best interests of his fellow workers.

"I ... I'm afraid I don't know enough about policy to be much help," was his bewildered argument.

"You know the difference between right and wrong," came back the heartening reply. "If you think anything is wrong, get up on your feet and say so!"

The convention wasn't long under way before a well-thought-out and carefully executed program of an anti-Christian minority group in the convention had progressed so far that its final adoption seemed a certainty. While most of the 1,600 assembled delegates (representing some 700,000 workers) sat back unaware that this small but influential bloc in their midst was on the brink of success, at the eleventh hour our friend — the one who didn't think he *knew* enough — got up from his chair.

He addressed the chairman, and was immediately recognized.

His mouth opened a couple of times to speak without giving forth a sound, but finally he managed, in a half-frightened voice, to say, *"I'm sorry, Mr. Chairman, but this whole thing doesn't seem honest to me!"*

Then he sat down quickly, mopping his forehead, feeling the blood pound madly through his veins, and waiting for the roof to fall in on him.

It fell in, all right — but not on him — because the effect of his simple statement on the rest of the gathering was electric. Up to then they had been quite passive, but now they came to life as if awakened from a deep sleep. A heated discussion followed. Eventually, realizing they had almost been railroaded into serious injustice, the delegates adopted a sound policy which was just the opposite of what the anti-Christians had cleverly proposed — and had almost got away with.

One man did all this, and one seemingly insignificant effort won a resounding victory.

Your individual power for good is no less than his, but you must not keep it to yourself. You must be honestly concerned about the salvation of all mankind, not merely absorbed in saving your own soul. You must fight where you can for the economic security of countless millions who can't fight for themselves. You must no longer remain aloof, utterly preoccupied with getting more and better food, housing, clothing, comforts and pleasures for yourself.

When a million like you do the same thing individually and collectively, it requires no great stretch of the imagination to realize what a far-reaching transformation can take place, not alone in America, but all over the world.

G.K. Chesterton spoke truly when he said that in spite of *all* accusations to the contrary, Christianity has not failed the world. The tragedy of our times is that too many have failed to try the truths of Christianity. Yet it is in *your* power to bring Christ back to the world and the world back to Christ. *You* have a touch of divinity which will begin to blossom into completeness here on earth, even before you hear those final words of eternal benediction:

"Come, you blessed of My Father. Receive the kingdom prepared for you from the foundation of the world" (Matthew 25:34).

CHAPTER NINE

Influencing From the Home

The home is the most vital social unit in any democracy. It influences the actions of all society. But goodness must not only be cultivated in the home, it must be carried far beyond its doors. And it is on the shoulders of those women who continue to choose the traditional role of homemaker that much responsibility falls — responsibility to your children, to your husband, to your neighbors and to yourself — of keeping the mainstream of life ever conscious of the great truths upon which civilization rests.

When you realize this and make it your business, in one way or another, to bring Christ into the marketplace, a fresh, purifying wind of lasting peace will sweep over this land. And eventually it will sweep on across the world! It will help everyone, even those extremists who are caught in the current widespread epidemic of sleeping tablet overdoses and lost weekends. Those sick with a nameless sense of guilt will want to keep on living, because from the home those women with a Christopher purpose will have made life worthwhile for the whole world.

Women Have the Power

Woman's influence for good can be great, but many women still underestimate their own power. You may feel bound down by the circumstances of everyday life. You might think you must be highly trained, have prominent positions, or be gifted with genius to do great things. Those may be your ideas, but they weren't Christ's! The woman of Samaria at Jacob's Well possessed none of these qualities, yet in her and through her Jesus brought untold numbers closer to His side. Peter and the other apostles and disciples were only ordinary men, usually unlettered and, more often than not, poor. Yet Christ said to them, *"Follow Me, and I will make you fishers of men"* (Matthew 4:19). And these common folk went on to revolutionize the entire world!

In every human being God has implanted, personally and individually, a special power to influence humankind for good. Those who understand this will become Christophers — Christ-bearers. And recognizing that same power in your spouse and in your children, you will inspire them to become Christ-bearers, too.

Give Your Family a Purpose

Then you will be less concerned that your sons and daughters choose profitable careers and more concerned that they find for themselves a sphere of influence for *good*. And insofar as you see them as instruments of God, you will automatically avoid that inclination of so many parents and teachers to overemphasize self-preservation, self-sanctification, self-development, and self-enjoyment — as if one's only purpose in life were to take care of his or her own soul and his or her own body, letting the rest of the world, literally and figuratively, "go to the devil." You will not imitate the wealthy parents of one young girl who taught their daughter from her earliest years to save every dollar she got her hands on, themselves matching every amount she so miserly amassed. These parents were not teaching her thrift. They were teaching her selfishness, a fact which showed itself later on in her self-centered life.

It's a fine thing to have security. But once that is achieved, then the first concern must be the food, housing, clothing, and education of others. It's a wonderful thing to know the truth. But you who possess the truth dare *not* leave the world in error. When true vision — Christ-like vision — is given to your children as they reach adulthood, they will not retire into their own insulated hothouses, into the cubicles of their faith, leaving the running of the big world to those who either hate Christ or know Him not. They will not devote themselves entirely to self-preservation, for any animal can do that. They will, instead, become other Christs, eager to help feed a hungry world, eager to help bring peace to a world divided against itself, eager to speak the truth to a world which has been too often listening only to lies.

You have a life ahead of you, and over the years, a thousand opportunities to train your children to be leaders, not followers; to choose a life's work not for the salary alone, but for the influence which that work affords. You cannot and dare not delegate that responsibility to others. The classroom cannot take the place of the home.

Aim for the Big Market

It's a big job, make no mistake about it. It's a challenge to all the best that is in you. But you can meet it, you must meet it, you will meet it. Unlike the woman in Washington, D.C., who listened to a Christopher talk and, while deeply impressed, still couldn't realize that she, personally, was capable of tremendous deeds, you will not ask as did she, "But couldn't you tell us some *little* thing to do?"

Good as she was, this woman was still thinking, as do too many otherwise fine people, in terms of little things, little projects, little spheres of influence — while the godless think in terms of the world!

The answer given her, however, opened her eyes to the breathtaking possibilities for good around her. "Here you are, living in the most important capital on the face of the earth," she was told, "with a thousand and one opportunities for doing something big, something worthwhile. Don't you see that? If a woman with your fine ideas were to spend a whole year getting just one decent, God-fearing person into some government job, you'd be doing a wonderful service to God and to your country! And remember this: even though you may think that you're just a little person, still you're important. You *count!*"

How well another woman, Mrs. Charlotte McDonnell Harris, realized the truth of this is evident from one very effective thing that she did. Some time ago she had read and been disturbed by an article in the *Ladies' Home Journal,* one of the country's leading women's magazines. This article, one in a series entitled "Letters to Joan," dealt with a so-called modern outlook on "sexual freedom in a changing world," with the implication that morals change with each generation. Others who read it may have shaken their heads, muttered to themselves, and then done nothing about it. But not Mrs. Harris. Her reply, "A Letter to Joan from a Catholic," appeared in a subsequent issue of the *Journal* despite the fact that she had never written for the general public before. She might easily have said, "Oh, but I can't. I'm no professional writer. Send it to the *Ladies' Home Journal?* Don't be silly. They wouldn't even read it, much less accept it!"

She might have said all these things, but she didn't. By her very silence she would have helped foster the continued publication of false concepts. And the significant thing about the whole affair is that the editors did read her article, sent her a nice check, and published what she had to say. As a result, her vital Christian message went out to some four and a half million homes. When it is remembered that not one of Christ's twelve apostles had the means of reaching any like number of people, then must come the realization of what wonderful things can be done from the home with the marvelous facilities of communication at your command. As the *Washington Post* pointed out not long ago, "The weakness of public opinion is that so many people express it only privately."

From the Home Into the Important Spheres

In the home and *from* the home, you can influence your family first of all, and second, the world outside. If there was a steady stream of young people from the average good American home entering the four great fields of education, government, labor-management and writing, it wouldn't take long to restore a healthy, wholesome tone to these important spheres of influence. In these spheres the bearers of Christ are most urgently needed.

In addition to those four main fields, there are others which offer splendid opportunities for Christopher work.

For instance, there are library and social service fields which are in serious need of representatives who have had deeply impressed upon them sound American principles. You can — and no doubt will — do much to answer that need as you grow in appreciation of the fact that there is little chance of Christ prevailing in the world until the homes which possess His peace share it with the world that does not.

"Every woman," to quote Pope Pius XII, "has then, mark it well, the obligation, the strict obligation in conscience, not to absent herself but to go into action in a manner and way suitable to the condition of each so as to hold back those currents which threaten the home, so as to oppose those doctrines which undermine its foundations, so as to prepare, organize and achieve its restoration."

"He Who Is Not With Me Is Against Me"

It is simply a choice of influencing or being influenced. And that last is the sad condition of millions of Americans who are not regularly reached by anyone in the name of Christ, leaving them openly susceptible to the half-truths and the deceiving glib come-ons of materialism. These people are living off the benefits of Christianity, but they are largely unaware of the major truths which are the basis of their liberties and which constitute the very foundation of our country. These truths are the chief obstacles to every subversive attempt to enslave our nation.

They have been stated earlier in this book, but fundamentals as important as these bear repeating so that your children may be enabled to know them. Briefly, they are: *belief* in a personal God; in Jesus Christ, true God and true man; in the Ten Commandments; in the sacred character of the individual; in the sanctity of marriage and the sanctity of the home as the basic unit of the human family; in the human rights of each person as coming from God, not from the State; in the right to private property with its consequent obligations; in due respect for domestic, civil and religious authority.

Finally, as a summation of all these, there should be emphasized a belief in judgment after death, when each individual must render an account of his or her stewardship to determine an eternity of Heaven or of Hell.

It won't do much good merely to be against those forces which would destroy our society. Too often all the countless discussions, all the club meetings, all the resolutions passed and sentiments expressed, unfortunately accomplish little. Too often do they add up to just one thing: *"Talk,* but no *action."* And just as actions do speak louder than any volume of words, so it is vital for each of you as Christophers to work as hard for Christ as His enemies are working against Him. Many among the millions of unchurched Americans are waiting, uncertain as to what road to take. It is up to you to begin to train your children now, so that they may become the Christophers of the future and carry on where you leave off. All your other activities, interesting as they may be, might well subordinate themselves to this one goal, because all those other activities rolled together will advance the free, God-given way of life very little.

True, all work and no play may make Jack a dull young man and Jane a dull young woman. But *all play* and *no work* for that which is just and good will leave the field clear to those intent on undermining our very civilization.

Take the Initiative

It is easy to fall into the attitude that changing times make it more difficult for succeeding generations to guard the sanctity of the home and to build strong and resilient families. It is easy to blame wars, depressions, booms, industrial and scientific revolutions as making much of American home life a weird and confused kind of existence.

It is our conviction, however, that this present dangerous trend can be reversed so that normal, healthy family life will once more take its place as the backbone of our civilization and bring an abundance of peace and happiness to the global community. To accomplish this means that the home will have to take the initiative and influence the world — instead of allowing itself to be influenced. Once you are convinced that it is much more hopeful and constructive to use every means possible to bring the peace of Christ that is in your home out into the mainstream of life, than to withhold it from the great majority who want and need it so much, then you will enthusiastically initiate from the sanctuary of your home many Christopher practices which will have an ever-widening influence for good.

To make this a reality, we submit a few proposals which you may find helpful:

1. Think in terms of the world. No matter how remote you may be from the marketplace, you can begin to reach out to all mankind. The very desire and attempt to do this will bring a blessing upon you, your home, and humanity. You will be imitating the world vision of Christ. Everything you do will take on new meaning, as it did for one stay-at-home mom who caught this perspective: "Thank you for inspiring an 'ingrown' homemaker, whose life has previously been bounded on all sides by homely details of child care and family feeding. Now I can see how this little world can take on new light as a fertile field for planting and living Christ for the bigger world. And so on from there!"

2. Pray for the world as well as for your home. The true Christopher will go far beyond the family circle with supplications to God. On the wings of prayer one can literally reach out over the globe itself. It is helpful to fix on particular intentions, a different one each day, each week, or each month if one chooses. Offering prayers for some specific purpose assures better continuity and greater sincerity. It isn't difficult to acquire the habit of offering a daily prayer for our President, for Congress, for the United Nations, for all who suffer because of their race, color or creed, for the billion and more men, women and children over the earth who have not yet heard that Jesus Christ was born, lived and died for each and every one of them. No particular form is necessary. You can make up your own prayer or use the following Christopher prayer:

"Inspire us, O God, with such a deep love of our country that we will be actively concerned in its welfare as well as in that of all our fellow countrymen for time and for eternity. Teach us to show by word and deed the same zealous interest in protecting and furthering the Christian principles upon which our nation is founded that others display in belittling or eliminating them.

"Guide and strengthen the President, his Cabinet, the members of Congress, the delegates to the United Nations, the Governor of our State, the officials of our community, and all others, in high position or low, who are entrusted with the task of protecting for all citizens those rights which come from You and from You alone.

"Teach us likewise to be worthy instruments in extending to all people of all nations, Your children and our brothers and sisters, the same peace, freedom and security with which You have so abundantly blessed our land. Through Christ Our Lord. Amen."

In the midst of your activities around the home you can say a passing prayer for all who died the day before. The obituary column in your morning paper can be your reminder for that. When you attend a movie, a football game, go to the beach or any other place where people congregate, take a moment to offer a prayer for all present. Eternity has begun for each of them, even though the majority never realize it. The more you pray for *everybody* — the poor, the rich, the strong, the weak, the friendly, the hostile, the wise, the stupid, the ugly, the fair — the more you will grow in love for them. You will experience a sense of participation with Christ in the salvation of the world that is possible in few other ways.

3. Dispose your children to lead lives of purpose. A tremendous change for the better would take place if one-quarter of the families in this country were to encourage at least one child in each family to dedicate a life to some career through which the best values learned from parents could be channeled to the "big market." Unfortunately and without intending any harm, many parents prepare their children for life pursuits that are discouragingly negative and restrictive. They fence them in as far as anything creative is concerned. They train them to be aimless followers rather than leaders. In a hundred ways they mold them to routine passiveness and to taking as much out of the world as possible; and, by implication at least, they give them to understand that they should not be overly concerned with putting anything in.

Even those parents with strong religious backgrounds are increasingly becoming entangled in the double game of trying "to serve God and mammon," with mammon slowly but surely winning out in their children, even more than in them. There is a tragic tendency to ignore the hidden power for good in each individual, and to deaden it if it does start to blossom forth. As a poor and harmful substitute, these same parents hold continually before their children's growing minds standards of worldly success — more money, better clothes, nicer homes, more expensive cars.

It would surprise those parents to know how often their offspring are disappointed in the lack of inspiration given them. Recently one young woman discovered a dangerous situation at a large teachers' college. This woman had the faith and ability to help remedy it. Yet, when asked why she didn't become a teacher herself, she replied, "I wanted to, but my mother and father told me to go and get a job where I could earn more money!"

For the first fifteen or twenty years of their lives, your children look to you for guidance, not only in the small things, but in the big things of life. You can train them to be Christ-minded or worldly-minded — both possibilities are there. It is up to you to set the pace and to point the proper direction. You can start improving the world, once you see in your own flesh and blood the best personal representatives you could ever have as Christophers. They will be the hope of the world when they, and enough more like them, get into the thick of things. And as they become active Christ-bearers, they will bring into the marketplace the goodness you passed on to them from God. These children of yours may some day touch the lives of countless persons as teachers, as government workers, as writers, as experts in the labor field, as librarians, and as social service workers — if you start right now to develop a missionary outlook within them.

4. Get into trends, national as well as local. No matter how little time you have to spare, try to use those moments on the bigger national projects as well as on those of your immediate environment. Don't, by any means, overlook local issues. They are important. But you will find that the more you interest yourself in the bigger problems, the more concerned you will be with the more important phases of local enterprises. Always remember that those who are against God are ever on the alert to poison the mainstream of life, knowing that the average person with religious convictions ordinarily moves in a very small sphere and shows little interest in bringing his or her principles to the marketplace.

For you this is as ringing a challenge as it was to a woman in Detroit, one afternoon not long ago. About to mail in her resignation to the Parent-Teacher Association, she happened to meet a friend who is a Christopher. After a brief conversation, the about-to-resign PTA member took the letter out of her purse and tore it up. "It never occurred to me that one person like myself mattered. But I see it now," she exclaimed.

If you join an organization or a club, make it one where you can do a little missionary work. Some of you can be more than mere members. You can get on committees, take official posts, and assume leadership in a variety of ways — not for personal advantage or privilege, of course, but with the distinct purpose of serving the general good.

Participate personally in all local, state and national elections, not only by voting but by getting others to vote as well, assisting them to reach a proper understanding of the issues at stake. Try to get full and authoritative information on candidates and all measures to be voted on sufficiently in advance so as to be able to take steps to see that this information is passed on to as many as possible.

Check into the teaching in all schools — elementary and high schools, colleges and universities — for which you are paying taxes. See that all teachers and instructors are upholding the Constitution as they have sworn an oath of allegiance to do. Whenever you find any defects, go yourself — and take others with you — to the school in question and request fulfillment of its obligation. It is usually more effective to go directly to the institution involved rather than to a board of education. Remember, this is your right, whether or not you have children in the school. As a taxpayer, the school is your concern as much as it is anyone's, and you, therefore, have a responsibility to it.

5. *Write letters.* This powerful means is at the disposal of every parent. (You will find suggestions about this in the following chapter, on letter-writing.) A habit easily formed, it is an excellent means of keeping alive a sense of participation in, and responsibility to, the big world that lies beyond the home.

One young mother, who does her bit by writing letters of approval or disapproval as part of her apostolate, told us, "I can't tell you how much I appreciate being a Christopher, even a silent one. Being the mother of two and expecting another, I'm tied to my home, but I'm still rarin' to do something concrete. I've had some interesting experiences in letter-writing, yet I never dreamed so much good could be accomplished with so little effort. I'm beginning to see more clearly than ever that all the household tasks in the world will matter little if we bury whatever other talents we have."

6. *Persuade others to be Christophers.* You will frequently find an opportunity to encourage at least one other person to be a doer, rather than a talker. It may be done by a word to your neighbor or to your grocer. It may be a note to your cousin in Wyoming, who hasn't decided what kind of a job to take after graduating from college. Or you may start things moving in the right direction simply by a conversation over the phone. One woman told how she

made a passing remark about a year ago in just that way. When a friend began bemoaning the confusion of the times, she countered with, "Well, I guess people like you and me can take our share of the blame. We want good government, good schools, good everything else, but we don't lift a finger to do anything about it. I can't think of one of our friends who is encouraging her kids to take any kind of a job except where they can feather their own nest." To this woman's amazement, six months later she learned that, as a result of her brief comment over the phone, her friend's son had taken a post on a board of education in Oregon and refused a tempting business offer which promised more money and a greater degree of financial security for the future.

7. Be selective and get others to be likewise. The fields of education, government, labor management, communications and other allied spheres that influence the thoughts and actions of millions, in the correct order of things should be your servants, not your masters. It is up to you to see that this order is not reversed. The best way to accomplish this is to see that these fields are staffed from top to bottom by normal, sensible Americans, rather than by those whose perverted reasoning is an ever-increasing threat to our democracy.

There is another means to achieve this purpose, however, and it is one that is not used often enough. It is your right to be selective, i.e., to *accept* what is good and *reject* what is evil. Most appreciate that they have a right of acceptance, but too often overlook their right of rejection. This distinction is most important. The apostles of atheism, subversion, perversion, viciousness, and rottenness of all types are forever abusing their God-given freedom to destroy freedom. Don't allow them to confuse you. Freedom must always be distinguished from license. One may be free to sell *good* oysters, but he has no right to sell bad ones.

From your home you have innumerable ways of exercising your right of acceptance and rejection. Do not worry about your sense of judgment. The average American mother and father are well blessed with common sense, fairness and safe norms of decency.

As citizens and as taxpayers, you can make your voices heard by insisting on truth and integrity in education and government and by taking steps to eliminate all that is opposed to them. With regard to the objectionable in newspapers, magazines, books, movies, radio and television, you can move mountains if you will but pass the word along and enlist, in every way you can, the cooperation of other parents. Censorship can be a dangerous means, but there is little chance of anything but good coming from the individual, personal judgment of people like you. By giving your patronage generously to what is good and withholding it from what you judge to be evil, you will be amazed at the vital power in your hands. The good you can do merely by not going to a movie that you think is below par, by turning off a television program that borders on the vulgar or subversive, by not buying a magazine which makes a policy of introducing stories or pictures that are out of place in your home, will be a revelation to you. If enough of your kind of people do that consistently and phone around the neighborhood to get other parents, who think similarly, to do the same, you will be starting a groundswell that cannot fail to have telling effects.

Yes, there are hundreds of ways in which you can start, as a committee of one, in being a Christopher in the sanctuary of your own home. You, and a million others like you, can develop together a force that nothing will be able to stop, that will sweep over the country and to the farthermost parts of the earth. You will have some inkling of the important role you are playing as a real partner of Christ in saving the world, a knowledge that will buoy you up in the midst of the difficulties that must be the lot of anyone who associates himself or herself in such an intimate relationship with the Crucified One. His lot was suffering from the crib to the cross, because He loved even the least of people so much. But you will never know, until you stand before the judgment seat of God, what your cooperation meant, how much you counted in bringing innumerable others to the heaven of happiness that Christ prepared for each and every human being. Then, in the perspective of eternity, you will see what a joy and a privilege it was to take things a bit hard on earth, in an attempt to make them a little easier for those who have not been blessed as have you.

Think Big and Act Big

But you will have to think and act in a big way — in terms of the world, not only of the neighborhood; of all people, not just a few. You will have to be daring and take literally the words of the Master when He said, "Launch out into the deep." In cautious, shallow water the returns are always small. Only far out in the deep, where the waves are rough and the chances great, is there much to be gained.

Rather than devote your time and energies to *theorizing* while the enemies of Christ are *doing*, rather than talk only to your own small circle while the godless talk to a hundred million others, rather than expend your lives in wishful thinking, in passing resolutions, or in complaining about conditions — with faith, with will, and with courage you can light your lantern and boldly carry it into the darkness of error and confusion and hate.

With God's help, you can bring the Christ-like qualities of the happy, Christian home back into a blind, unhappy world. Like Our Lady — the first Christ-bearer — literally and figuratively you can help renew the face of the earth.

For all of you there is a breathtaking opportunity, a tremendous challenge. There is no time to lose. Already too long on the march, the forces of evil have ravaged half the globe. With quick daring, however, and by acting at once, you can stop that march. You can be God's means — God's servants — in restoring to a weary, heartsick world the peace for which Christ suffered and died!

CHAPTER TEN

Letter Writing

A Service to Society

Letter writing — intelligent letter writing with a constructive message — is a very important service in preserving the God-given liberties of our free society. The letter you write *today* may do much to preserve tomorrow your own home and the homes of families a thousand miles away. Indeed, a letter is a form of life insurance for our nation.

Persons in positions of responsibility — legislators, newspaper and magazine writers, motion picture producers and broadcast network directors — are much more susceptible to public opinion than is generally realized. One of the outstanding Hollywood motion picture reporters stated recently that the effect of constructive letters has been to change for the better much of the content of her movie gossip columns. Mothers and fathers all over the country, it appears, had written so many letters to her, protesting in a friendly but determined way about the strengthening of the trend towards divorce through constant references to Hollywood marital breakups, that she finally came to see the importance and reasonableness of their opinions.

In *Reader's Digest,* a California Congressman recently pointed out that every morning at ten o'clock in our nation's capital finds all our Representatives and Senators doing the same thing: *reading their mail.* "Congressmen may miss committee meetings," he said, "absent themselves from the floor, fail to show up for roll calls and votes. But they always read their mail."

From their mail, the Congressman continued, our Representatives in Washington know what the people back home want and expect. Yet it must not be thought that they simply take the total number of letters for an issue and the total against the same issue and decide which is the heavier pile. "One thoughtful letter will outweigh half a dozen which simply say 'vote for this' or 'vote for that'," he said. "One spontaneous outburst on your own stationery is worth a hundred copies of someone else's letter or newspaper clippings in some write-your-Congressman drive."

One man who has been in Congress for ten years says that the letters which really count are those that show your legislative representative three things: (1) that it is you yourself doing the writing, (2) that you know something about the subject, (3) that you have done some thinking. "If every voter wrote one letter like that once a year," says the legislator, "I believe we'd have a fifty percent better Congress."

The power of a good letter, therefore, should never be underestimated. A single letter — sometimes even a brief note — has been known to change the course of life for many a man and woman. A few good letters, timely and sincere, have been able to influence the thinking of millions.

Making Your Opinion Heard

Many people fail to write letters because they have the attitude "What good will it do? What's done is done."

How faulty this reasoning is can best be illustrated by what one leading network executive said in defending the type of programs he aired to the public. "If you don't get all the educational programs you want," he said in effect, "if you don't get the kind of music you like, the kind of comedy, mystery story, soap opera or whatever else you wish, it's your own fault. We listen to our audience. They make our programs."

The power you can exert, not only in broadcasting but in all spheres of influence once you become articulate was well illustrated not long ago by what happened to a chain of motion picture theaters in the Midwest. This particular theater chain made no distinction in the sort of programs they showed on Friday evenings and the features they displayed on Saturday afternoons for children. One mother thought there should be a distinction. She thought weekend movies ought to be adapted to the needs of the children who attended in large numbers. "You ought to have pictures more suitable for youngsters," she wrote the head of the theater chain. "Instead of glamor and the gunplay of gangsters, why not substitute wholesome films — some of the better westerns, for example? Or travelogues or comedies? Youngsters oughtn't to be exposed to the atmosphere of the roadhouse, the police blotter, the divorce court. They shouldn't spend several hours of their time each week seeing pictures which instill in them unrealistic desires for slick limousines, penthouses and lives of ease and luxury, as so many current movies do. Such films only give them a false perspective of life...."

The management brushed the letter aside, as the theater executive frankly admitted. "Just let her cool off," was his terse comment. "She'll forget the whole thing."

But the woman didn't forget. She wasn't a crank, and she wouldn't be ignored. Off she went to the two groups in her hometown to which she belonged — a Catholic society and a civic garden club. She tackled her friends in both organizations, urging them to write to the management. She recommended that their letters be brief, courteous, and *firm*.

The reaction to these public expressions of opinion was not long in coming. Such a volume of letters poured in that the management reluctantly decided to shift over temporarily to the kind of pictures requested, though they were "fully convinced" the proposition wouldn't work. Attendance would drop off, they said. They'd lose money and with it their reputation for being smart businessmen.

But things turned out quite differently from what they expected. "We not only make everybody happy," the head of the theater chain exclaimed afterwards, "but we make much more money under the new arrangement, as a matter of fact, than we did under the old."

In Rochester, N.Y., a young high school girl recently wrote the editor of that city's newspaper:

> "All of us have been reading lately of the shocking rise in the divorce rate. Too little is being done to correct the situation. Novels and the motion pictures furnish us with escapist literature, when what is needed is something to bring us sharply to our senses, and help keep a sacred ceremony from becoming a pitiful farce."

The student went on to advocate the use of all means possible to emphasize and make Americans aware of the sacredness and dignity of marriage and the vows they had sworn to keep.

The letter so impressed the editor than he declared in an editorial:

> "A contributor to our Readers' Forum today has a suggestion that should not be allowed to go the way of yesterday's newspaper. It cries for action. Divorce and tandem marriages are glamorized on every hand. A few weeks ago the idols of American Youth in two of their top interests ran off with other men's wives and, after hasty divorces, married them. Society must do something to make youths believe in marriage.

"Our correspondent may not have the whole answer. But it is an idea that should be kicked around and looked at from all angles until a scheme that can be realized comes out of it."

The letter of a woman office worker from Buffalo, N.Y., on a particularly necessary piece of legislation up for Congressional consideration won a public tribute from one of the state's Senators for the woman's interest. Not only that, she was instrumental in prodding thousands of her fellow citizens to make their voices heard in favor of the measure. When questioned as to why she had written her letter in the first place, she simply replied, *"I'm a Christopher."*

Preliminary Preparation for Good Letter Writing

In letter writing, as in any other kind of writing, there are certain preliminary rules, which anyone who hopes to persuade others to see the point he or she is trying to make would do well to follow.

First of, there is the *remote preparation.* This consists of (1) observation, (2) reading, and (3) reflection.

Anyone can train his or her powers of *observation* and learn to see accurately and to retain what he or she sees. The importance of *reading* what goes on in the world in newspapers, in books and in magazines hardly needs any emphasis. In addition to being a valuable aid in letter writing, it is one of the contributing factors to a well-rounded education. Observation and reading are of little use, however, unless people acquire the habit of *reflection* on what has been observed and read. The man or woman who does not reflect, as Cardinal Newman said, sees "the tapestry of human life as it were on the wrong side, and it tells no story."

Though not a technical rule like those of observation, reading and reflection, being sincere is just as important to good letter writing. We will never succeed in influencing others through our letters if, in order to make an impression, we pretend to possess what we do not actually have. We should stick to the facts and express our own honest feelings.

Specific Laws to Follow

All writing — letter writing, essay writing, book writing, short story or novel writing — is based on four fundamental laws: (1) unity, (2) coherence, (3) emphasis, (4) interest.

Unity means that the letter must be about one thing, just as good business practice insists that commercial correspondence limit itself to one topic in each exchange of notes. Unity is achieved without too much effort simply by asking oneself the question, "What do I want to say?" before taking pen in hand or sitting down at the keyboard. Failure to ask this question is responsible for the greatest number of mistakes in any sort of writing.

For your letter to have *coherence,* one part should follow after another, logically and naturally. Material should be arranged so that its order of importance is apparent to the reader. Some parts of your letter, of course, will be more important than others and so you will want to make certain things stand out.

This involves what is known as positioning ideas which, properly done, makes for *emphasis.* People tend to remember most what comes at the beginning and what comes at the end of any piece of writing. If anything, the last thought expressed is remembered best of all (but an effort should be made to have letters so interesting that readers will read to the end). The *proportion* of space you devote to any one idea is quite likely to be the measure of how much you want to impress that idea on those who read your letter.

The most effective way to capture the readers' *interest* is to use concrete matters freely. Examples, illustrations, comparisons, stories, descriptions, factual reference from newspapers, magazines, etc., will aid in this. They will help to rivet the attention of the reader to the ideas you wish to put across. The dull letter seldom succeeds in impressing anyone.

Give yourself to your letters. Understand what you are writing about. Gather sufficient evidence to support the point you are trying to make. Present your ideas attractively.

Be brief, but not curt. Use a moderate tone in all your letters. Friendly, constructive criticism (if that is your intention) will accomplish far more than angry outbursts. It is the old story — mentioned elsewhere in this book — of "disagreeing without being disagreeable." The head of an eastern manufacturing concern, who wrote to one of the movie studios regarding a picture he felt put crime in a too-favorable light, illustrates the point very well. After commending the studio for its efforts in the past to keep its entertainment standards high, he stated in detail his objection to the film in question. And he concluded with these well-chosen words:

"If I am wrong, please overlook this letter; if I am right, I am happy to be able to call your attention to what must be an oversight of your splendid organization."

Regarding the technical construction of your letter, it is suggested that you make an outline if it is at all possible. It will help you follow the laws of good letter writing.

Keep your paragraphs short, three to five sentences, and your sentences correspondingly brief, fifteen to twenty-five words. Use language with which your reader will be familiar. Avoid slang or trite, hackneyed phrases. Whenever possible, begin with an anecdote, a case history, or by posing a problem. End with a summary and make your last sentence one that will linger in your reader's mind. One authority sums this all up in these words: "Logical organization, avoidance of cliches and jargon, adequate transitional aids, and other such rhetorical maneuvers will help marvelously in sustaining reader interest. But in my opinion the two stylistic devices which most contemporary editors are seeking are *conversational quality* and *concreteness*."

You may not always be writing to an editor, of course, but these rules apply whether you are writing to a publication, to your congressional or local legislative representative, to a radio or TV station or motion picture studio, or to some organization or society. These rules are not arbitrary enactments of grammarians. They are based upon sound psychology — upon an insight into human nature. And, in writing letters, it is human nature with which you have to deal. As for style, fundamentally any particular approach to writing is but a thinking-out put into language. Providing you mean what you say and say what you mean, there will not be any need for striving after an effect. Pretentiousness here, as anywhere else in life, may antagonize rather than persuade.

Write a Note of Appreciation

In all this discussion on good letter writing with a constructive message, there should be mentioned an additional type of correspondence which is almost equally important, namely, the note of appreciation.

People and organizations welcome constructive criticism and suggestions. A letter of praise for a job well done is a powerful stimulant for persevering effort along the same lines.

Even a brief note of encouragement often has far-reaching results. Among the thousands of messages which poured into the American Broadcasting Company not long ago, praising a documentary presented by the network, was this note of appreciation from a listener: "…[this program] was brilliantly written and produced and a special tribute to your courage and vision. As a sincerely appreciative American, may I earnestly hope that this is only the beginning of many many more of this same type program under your completely able guidance. May God bless you in all your undertakings."

Letters like this are incentives to continue the good work in the future. Here are four reactions to such notes sent by Christophers. All are in similar vein. Yet even in the slight variation of the wording all show a profound sense of gratitude that people have taken the time to inform them of their interest.

"Greatly appreciated your letter," wrote one leading columnist to a reader. *"I get my share of unfavorable mail, so letters like yours are doubly welcome."*

"I appreciate the encouragement we receive in letters like yours," was the grateful acknowledgment of a school superintendent to a public-spirited correspondent.

From a weekly news magazine to a letter writer who praised the publication for a splendid article: *"Thank you very much for your warming note.... Showed it to all hands concerned and they were naturally much pleased."*

"It is most heartening to know," replied one prominent official in the State Department to a correspondent, *"that I have your support in undertaking what promises to be a difficult although interesting assignment...."*

Of course, it is quite possible that you may not receive any reply to the letters you have sent to editors, government officials, civic leaders and others. Don't be surprised at this. Persons in such positions are usually so deluged with work that no matter how impressed they may be with what you have to say, they often have neither the time nor the facilities to tell you so. However, your letter *registers,* even if they cannot thank you for it.

One of America's foremost magazines, with a tremendous circulation, passes through thirty-five different hands every constructive letter received. Even if a letter is utterly opposed to their editorial policy, it receives the same attention they give to pleasant notes of commendation.

So whether you do or do not receive an answer matters little.

What does matter is that you are on the alert, reaching others with sound, healthy ideas. Your letters, you may be sure, are read. And they do have their effect.

One Letter a Week

You could easily write one letter a week, whether it be of praise or of constructive criticism. In some instances, you might even be able to write one good letter a day. All it takes is a few minutes of your time. And all you have to do to make sure your letter is a good letter is to remember these principles: (1) write as you would to a friend — be personal, not impersonal; (2) be constructive, not destructive; (3) be specific, not vague; (4) make your point but don't keep repeating it; (5) be brief, but not curt; (6) be yourself, think for yourself, write for yourself; (7) write as you would talk; (8) offer a positive suggestion, don't just complain; (9) inject a friendly feeling along with the facts; (10) be neat and be sure to sign your name and address clearly. Anonymous letters, or those without addresses, are simply disregarded.

Like the young woman in Buffalo who, when asked why she wrote the original letter that had such a ripple effect, replied, "I'm a Christopher," you can make the thoughts you put down on paper perform a real service to society. As a Christopher, you have the responsibility to express your opinion on every subject which affects you and your neighbors. By the few lines you may send to some newspaper, some movie studio or television station, to some local or national legislator, you may be the means of bringing untold numbers that much nearer to the God-given principles on which our republic is founded. And you may likewise bring untold numbers to a better appreciation of the Truth for which Christ suffered and died.

CHAPTER ELEVEN

To Business Leaders — A Challenge

The tremendous impact for good one businessman made on the lives of thousands was well illustrated recently in the farewell tribute paid him following his untimely death. These eloquent words appeared in a secular publication devoted to the interests of labor:

"The death of Basil Harris, president of the U.S. Lines, removes a Catholic landmark from the New York waterfront. He knew the shipping business and made it a profitable enterprise. For this his associates honored him and sought his counsel.

"But the men who went down to the sea in his ships, the men and women working in his offices, the longshoremen and the union officials, all these respected and honored him for much better reasons. 'He was a man of his word,' they said — fair and square, a man who never belittled any man by his wealth or power.

"The inspiration of his life was Christ and he served Him well. All the titles and dignities that honored him meant little to him; indeed, it was he who distinguished them. He would have rejoiced with a great-hearted laugh at the way the announcement of his death was received in a waterfront bar. The Tussler pushed his cap back, drenched the news with his beer. 'God, that was a good guy!' The gang's 'Yep' would have sounded better to Basil Harris than any choir's amen."

The 1,500 persons who attended Mr. Harris' funeral included very many business leaders, to be sure. But a far greater number of stevedores, dock men, teachers, caddies, grocers, taxi drivers, gardeners, policemen, office help and others came to bear witness to their love and affection for one who had, at all times, given those very things to each of them.

In many ways Mr. Harris was a Christopher. Love of all people, the distinguishing mark of the true Christ-bearer, was certainly a part of him. Many know of the generosity he displayed in sharing his material possessions, but only a few are aware of his countless daily acts of kindness to those who needed and wanted more than money. He was motivated from within by some greater power than mere human philanthropy, an activity all too seldom accompanied by personal solicitude. The most significant tribute, perhaps, that could be paid him was the quiet service he rendered during the Great Depression. Countless unemployed men and women who sought desperately for jobs found, when they approached Harris, the helping hand they needed. "I don't know of anyone who has gone to him in search of a job that he hasn't helped get one," an associate of his commented at the time. "I take my hat off to him. Most of us give money, but Basil does that and more. He gives his time. He gives himself!"

The driving force back of all this was a deep spiritual sense which had been stimulated while Harris was a student at Princeton University. One evening near the end of the school term he visited three classmates who roomed together, in order to go over some examination material with them. After a couple of hours of study one of them decided to go to bed earlier than the others. He said good night, and then went off to his corner of the room. Once into his pajamas, he knelt down and, for about ten minutes, recited the Rosary.

This simple expression of faith made a lasting impression on Harris, and during his lifetime he referred back to it continually.

As for the student, little did he realize that what he had done was to be the turning point in the life of one of his companions. Years later Basil Harris became a Catholic and from then on his entire outlook was dominated by a devotion to God that was strong, resourceful, deep and constant.

Unlike many other successful business people whose very expressions betray preoccupation with power and wealth, Harris displayed a wonderful sense of humor and gaiety. He took pleasure in giving others pleasure. He was particularly kind and cheering to the poor who often get the least personal attention.

Wealth, as such, meant little to him, and his feeling in this regard was well expressed in a remark he made one day while en route from Washington to New York. Reading in the paper about a millionaire who had just died as he was in the process of building a large new estate, he exclaimed:

"That sounds like the fellow in the Gospel — the one who pulled down his barns to build bigger ones and forgot he was to appear before God that very night for the final payoff."

At the other end of the economic ladder, a small businessman, a tinsmith in New York, saw his goal in life with the same clear vision as did Basil Harris. The purpose of this tinsmith, one Paul Antonio, was to make the world a little better than he found it. Because he tried to think and act in terms beyond the confines of his own small shop, one thing in particular that he did bears mentioning now.

Some time back he was hired to build and install the black steel ballot box which is now used by members of the Security Council of the United Nations when they cast their votes. When the box was opened just before the first Security Council session, there at the bottom was a brief message written in clear handwriting on a cheap piece of notepaper. The message read:

> "May I, who have had the privilege of constructing this ballot box, cast the first vote? May God be with every member of the United Nations Organization, and through your noble efforts bring lasting peace to us all — all over the world.
>
> (signed) "Paul Antonio, mechanic."

By this one simple act did Antonio give the Council members a reminder of the importance of the supernatural. At the same time (because the incident was widely publicized for its human interest angle) he got the same lesson over to millions in our land and over the world.

The Proper Approach

There are many business people who feel and act as did Paul Antonio and Basil Harris. But there are many, many more — and these constitute the majority — on whom a God-given concept of human existence has not made a sufficient impression. These people are good, solid citizens, however. They stand for law and order. They are a credit to their community. But, unfortunately, they often *underestimate the power for good* which they could exert on a large scale. They restrict themselves, in so many ways, to spheres that are local and small. They do not participate actively and in great numbers to influence for the better, as surely as they could, the trends that convulse mankind today. Theirs is the lack of recognition of the "truths that make men free."

They may acknowledge that the world is sick, yet too often they neglect to do what is only ordinary common sense to cure its ills. And by their neglect they leave the field to those who have a well-calculated, carefully prepared plan to revolutionize the earth and reshape it in the form of a totalitarian, godless global state.

A French businessman who visited this country not long ago made a statement which illustrates this situation in all its stark reality.

"My interests were limited to my business, my house, my weekends," this Frenchman said. "I paid no attention to our government, our schools, our labor movements. I found out rather late that those who were very much interested in every phase of France's public life were men whose one evil objective was to wreck our country. That they have nearly succeeded is due to the neglect of men like myself to give time and intelligent effort to what concerns the common interests of all. It was my mistake as a businessman. I hope American businessmen do not make the same mistake."

American business people *have been* making that mistake, unfortunately. Their handicap has been that too often they have identified themselves with things, rather than with *ideas.* They do everything possible for the comfort and convenience of the body, forgetting that the totalitarians hit first, last and always for the intellect and soul of each and every man, woman and child.

By the very nature of his or her calling, a businessman or woman should be a force for good in and far beyond the local community. Yet, of all groups of people, as one business firm itself pointed out, "businessmen are most laggard in their interest in the exchange of ideas."

Good Deeds Wasted

Often a business leader will give a new wing to a college or university and yet have little or no idea what will be taught there. Not infrequently, the very principles for which he or she stands will be undermined in those classrooms.

Again, with but few exceptions, the huge foundations created by prominent business leaders are confined to the physical and material, seldom to the development and furtherance of the basic principles on which our country, *as a free democracy,* exists.

From one end of this country to the other, tens of thousands of our finest citizens are engaged in various forms of small business. These people constitute part of the backbone of our nation, but their primary preoccupation is with the *small* problems in their midst. Meanwhile they are being saturated with poisonous ideas by others who, daringly bold, are gambling for big stakes and are playing for keeps.

These doers of evil are not outsiders. They are part of our American society. With amazing prophetic accuracy, in the nineteenth century the great British historian and statesman, Lord Macauley, pointed that out.

"Your republic," he said, "will be pillaged and ravaged in the twentieth century, just as the Roman Empire was by the barbarians of the fifth century, with this difference: the devastators of the Roman Empire came from abroad, while your barbarians will be the people of your own country and the products of your own institutions."

Concept of God Ignored

Most thinking people are aware that some sort of a breakdown along these lines is going on in America. What they don't seem to realize, however, is that probably the greatest single factor in the rise of the godless philosophy of totalitarianism comes from allowing the concept of God to fall into disuse. Some business leaders have lost all sense of the Brotherhood of Man under the Fatherhood of God. They have lost the realization that every human being is a child of God, made in His own image and likeness. One British colonial industrialist not long ago expressed the tragedy of this attitude when he said:

"There was a time when I might have been interested in helping poor devils in need. Once I even thought of building a hospital out here for the study of tropical diseases. But I kept putting it off until I had more time and money. When I began in this hole, I was going to quit as soon as I had ten thousand pounds. When I got that, I decided to make it twenty. Then I went on piling up money until it was too late; the stuff had buried me!"

This man had lost contact with humankind. In the tired, slow shake of his head as he spoke, it was obvious that he was alone, and fated forever to remain so unless he made a sincere effort to regain his sense of perspective, to regain the true belief that fame and fortune in this life are fleeting and the things of Heaven are not.

The Situation Is Not Hopeless

This man's case — and thousands like his — are not hopeless, however. There is still time (though the hour is growing late) to get "back on God's side." But people of good will must be more than just against past personal evils and present public ones, such as Communism, or Nazism, or Fascism. All these evils spring out of warped attempts to correct abuses and right wrongs. And even if all these philosophies were suddenly eliminated, the principal problem would still remain, that of the godless materialism which is the cancer in the life of America. Just as disease strikes, not because of the power of the germ but because of the lowered resistance of the body, so a great many otherwise good people who have scarcely a speaking acquaintance with first principles are becoming easy targets for many popular errors.

Sound-thinking, God-fearing people must be for something; they must be for the daily application of all the God-given principles upon which this country is founded.

Business people could be the shock troops of these good ideas once they see that it is from ideas alone that the great forces in the world, good as well as evil, proceed. If they will apply the same ingenuity and devotion to the spreading of good, sound American ideas that they apply to their own private pursuits, they can arrest and change for the better — more effectively, perhaps, than any other group — the disintegrating process that is menacing more and more the best interests of our country and our civilization. Business leaders striving personally and individually, however, can easily bring about a change for the better if they will devote a comparatively small part of their time and effort, and perhaps no more than one-tenth of the money now being expended on their present charities, to preserve and spread the fundamental American principles which make their business, their private pursuits, the very life of their nation, possible.

To their credit, more and more business and professional people are beginning to realize their responsibilities and, more significantly, are beginning to do something about it. One zealous Christopher, an Indiana lawyer, drew up with a group of friends an advertisement and arranged for it to be given eye-catching space in daily newspapers in the Middle West. Though it appeared only once, it brought home to countless readers a positive fact of which many of them are losing sight and of which they need to be reminded.

The ad called on those who read it to remember the "basic principles of Americanism" enunciated in the Declaration of Independence, and then quoted from that document to spell them out. It continued:

"Thus, as a good American, you must believe that:

1. God is the Creator of all men.
2. Your rights and the rights of your fellowmen are God-given, and *for that reason alone* no power on earth can take these rights away.
3. As a personal creature of God, each of us is equal in the sight

of God to every other person, and *for that reason* each of us is entitled to the equal protection of all the laws in the land.

4. Government is not man's master; on the contrary, government is man's servant, chosen by man to protect the God-given rights of mankind.

"Upon the firm foundation of these truths the glory and prosperity of our beloved country has risen steadily through the years to be the crowning wonder of the world. These truths have made America great. Only these truths can keep America great. If you want to be a good American and preserve the blessings of liberty for yourself and your posterity, then — hold these truths."

Emulating the examples of the Indiana lawyer and his associates, a group of business people and newspaper officials in the Midwest have embarked upon a campaign to get service clubs and parent-teachers organizations in states not requiring the study of the Declaration of Independence to correct this condition at once. Further, they have set up a program urging the head of the household to read the Declaration, and the Preamble to the Constitution, to the entire family on the Fourth of July.

In similar vein, a paper company in Indianapolis announced its determination to work for a wider recognition of the basic American doctrine which is the heritage of free men in a free society. "We hear a great deal these days about various 'plans' — the 'Five Year Plan,' the 'Marshall Plan,' and many others," this company wrote. "We think it is well for us to give heed to another 'plan' adopted July 4, 1776 — the Declaration of Independence. We have had copies of this prepared and are enclosing one herewith."

In addition to these methods of bringing to public consciousness our priceless, God-given heritage, many business leaders have also found other means of getting into the mainstream of life the sound ideas whose widespread distribution will do much to preserve our free way of life. In some cases they have done this personally. In other cases where they have been unable to get into the thick of things themselves, they have encouraged and actively assisted others to go into the marketplace. Some of these enterprising people hold prominent positions in industrial and financial life. Others are less in the public spotlight.

A stockbroker in upper New York State has encouraged his two daughters to become teachers and his son to go into government service — with a Christopher purpose.

A forty-six-year-old Cincinnati businessman gave up a well-salaried manufacturing position to prepare to join a college faculty where he can teach American government. He claims as the motivating reason for this step the deep impression made upon him by many young people "who want to participate in politics but don't know what to do." And he continued, "When I decided to go back to school after being away for twenty-six years, I was afraid my friends and business colleagues would think I was crazy or something. I was astonished to discover that ninety percent of them — many of whom I thought were only interested in making an honest buck — considered it a wonderful idea and wished they could do the same."

A businessman in Boston is currently helping his son in all the necessary preparation required prior to his entering the labor relations field.

A public accountant who assisted his son to follow a career as a film scenario writer has seen his interest pay dividends a thousand times over in several outstanding motion pictures this young man has already helped prepare.

An insurance agent, part of a firm which employs some one thousand persons, is acting as a committee of one to step up interest among the workers about getting better-quality Americans into the four spheres which mainly influence our lives today — education, government, labor-management and communications.

A lawyer who found himself, in his own words, "getting so wrapped up in law practice I've been overlooking the more important things in life," has completed plans to go into government service with a Christopher motive in mind.

An official in a large New York publishing concern goes on record with the following:

"Last year I was asked to consider running for my local school board but I decided against it. Later, when I mentioned my refusal to a Christopher friend of mine, he told me it was my duty to run. So this year when a similar request was made of me, recalling his advice, I did run and was elected. Now that I'm on the board I can tell you I never realized there could be so many wonderful opportunities to further fundamental American principles. My only regret is that I didn't realize it sooner."

As soon as there are more people like these "turning on lights" in our country than there are enemies "turning them off," then and then only will the "darkness" begin to vanish.

Same Methods — A Different Goal

In a specific way, business leaders can learn from the godless how they carry their ideas into every field in which they can reach the most people; how they put thousands of their *missioners* into all fields that sway men's thoughts and actions.

And as business people pattern their *procedure* after the godless — but with a different goal and a different motive — as they inspire tens of thousands of Americans to dedicate themselves to the task of bringing into every phase of public and private life the idea that there is a personal God, that man is more than an animal, and that all the rights he has have their origin in, and depend upon, the Almighty, they will restore a sense of personal responsibility and individual accountability as an integral part of American life.

The sobering effects of such a task are well emphasized in a passage from *The Late George Apley* where a father, speaking to his son, said:

> *"In a sense we are all servants, placed here on earth to serve. Some of us, by the will and omniscience of the Divinity, have been given a greater task than others; I count myself, somewhat to my sorrow, as a member of that group. It is a very grave thought to me to think that I may soon have to render an account of my stewardship to my Maker. I have held control of some large industries in this country and through them I have controlled the lives of many people. This is a solemn thought and someday it will be a solemn thought for you. There are certain definite obligations for one in my position and one in yours — and one of them is to try and make your life worthwhile with the advantages God has given you."*

Such realization, belated as this man's was, is a wonderful thing. But similar realization in all spheres of our national life must come, and come quickly, if we are to avoid disaster. Make no mistake about it. The twentieth century has brought into being for the first time in all history a vigorous, aggressive, ruthless crusade to spread evil from one end of the earth to the other. It is global in scope, and it is here to stay. It is spreading with astonishing speed; it is ever on the march. By its deceptive and destructive allurements, it has already blighted, poisoned, and enslaved hundreds of millions of people.

Business leaders can do much to change this trend. And it will be a glorious thing if these same people, who accomplished so much to win the recent war, will go one step further and help win the peace for which the world still longs. And that peace will come only when the basic idea on which our country was founded — that man gets his rights not from the State but from God —

becomes a world reality. The problem of bringing this about is largely one of *distributing* or merchandising the basic idea.

Since, by the very nature of their work, business people must be specialists in distribution and experts in merchandising, they should inevitably succeed in seeing that this fundamental idea is given wide circulation and thorough integration into every phase of American life. Considerable experimentation has proved this can be done with relative ease. All over the country thousands of Christophers — Christ-bearers — have been encouraged to go into the four important phases of public life and have been encouraged to show the same determination in restoring basic *Christian* ideas as others are displaying in throwing them out. The success of these Christopher business people in every field is living proof of what can be done. All that remains is to increase the number of distributors of good ideas. Those in the business world can certainly be effective Christophers themselves; and, by the same token, they can and must get others, *many others,* to be Christ-bearers.

There is no time to lose. Things are moving fast. It is either lead or be led, influence or be influenced. To survive individually, one must strive persistently in helping all to survive. Now, as never before, it is "one for all and all for one."

As business leaders rise to this glorious challenge of spreading ideas, as we know they can, the prospects for peace will begin to glow ever brighter. But nothing — nothing — must be taken for granted. Success will be directly proportionate to their thinking in terms of *all* people, not merely a few; in *ideas,* not merely things; as they give *themselves,* not merely their money; as they take the effective measures to circulate *good* ideas, not merely watch passively from the sidelines.

As business people — as Christophers — do all these things, it will be living, inspiring proof that they need not *"be overcome by evil, but overcome evil by good"* (Romans 12:21).

CHAPTER TWELVE

Young People

A Big Job Ahead

One hot early summer afternoon several years ago on a high school baseball diamond in a New England town, Bill Daley, a wiry, laughing youngster of fifteen, stood on the sidelines squinting into the sun, watching his teammates stepping up to the plate to take their cuts in pregame batting practice.

His eyes were shining, his lips drawn slightly apart with excitement, his body tensed as he took in every move his companions made. For baseball was his love, his whole life. Had you asked, at the drop of a hat he could have given you the batting and fielding averages of every well-known big leaguer. And had you asked, also, what was his ambition in life, he'd have told you simply: "To play baseball as a pro. You know, in the big time!"

Bill Daley never realized his ambition. After that particular day he was never to play another game of any kind in his life. Before the afternoon was half over he was lying in a hospital, victim of an accident on the field about which he has only the haziest recollection beyond the fact that somehow during the game he fell and landed heavily on his back. When he tried to rise, he found he couldn't move. There was a strange numbness in his legs and a tightness in his back that sent cold sweat pouring down his face, smarting his eyes, salting his mouth as he bit his lip to keep from crying out in panic.

At the hospital the doctors were friendly and very kind. He'd suffered a spinal injury, they told him, but added that he wasn't to worry. They'd do everything in their power to help him.

But as the weeks went by and became months and, finally, years, and their efforts proved to be in vain, Bill had to acknowledge to himself what was to be his lot in life — not only that he would never walk again, but that he would spend his life in bed.

Many a boy would have been tempted to turn against the world for the way it had cheated him out of all the good things to which a lad of his age had a right to look forward — the ball games, the hikes, the swimming and campings-out during the summer vacations, the weekly trips to the local movie house, all the hundred and one things a healthy, active youngster does.

High Purpose in a Changed Body

It is to Bill's credit that after the first terrible shock had passed, he made himself accept his fate, refusing to feel sorry for himself. If things were to be this way, well, okay, he'd make the best of them. He wasn't the first boy to lose the ability to walk, and he would not be the last. After all, he'd had fifteen years in which to race around. Some kids he'd read about never even had that long.

That was seventeen years ago. From that day to this, Bill Daley has never been able to move off his back. For a long time now he hasn't even been able to turn over and lie on his side because of the pain from rheumatoid arthritis which has developed. "I don't mind," Bill will tell you. "I decided long ago after this happened to stop thinking of myself and devote the rest of my life to making the world a better place than I found it."

A cynic might have laughed at that, though not to Bill's face, of course. After all, what *could* someone like him do? Why, he couldn't even take care of himself, let alone do anything for anyone else. But, like the bird whose wingspread is such as to defy the laws of aerial motion (according to scientists), yet being unaware of the fact, *flies,* Bill never has recognized his situation as an obstacle to completing what he set out to do.

To keep his mind occupied, he studied short-wave radio and then received an amateur radio operator's license. Using his own equipment, he kept in touch with ham operators all over the world, listening to their chatter, sometimes to their personal troubles, giving his advice, yet never once mentioning his own condition. When World War II came along, he volunteered his services as a radio operator and was accepted by the Coast Guard to monitor and intercept, from his home, any enemy signals he could pick up from the Nazi submarines or surface craft which might approach the American coast, with instructions to relay such signals to Coast Guard headquarters. Bill did a tremendous job, as those familiar with the case have stated many times.

When the war ended, he found his real vocation in life. In 1946, after learning about the plans of the Christophers soon to get under way, he set about spreading their idea by mail. Together with this he became active in everything aimed at the good of others. From his bedside in a small, unpretentious flat where he lives with his mother, sister and blind father, there have poured out hundreds and thousands of pamphlets, booklets, clippings, and news notes which he had asked to be sent in bulk to his home. And from all over the country and even from overseas, came messages from people in all walks of life, telling him how much what he was doing meant to them, never suspecting for a moment that this human dynamo correspondent of theirs was paralyzed.

When you ask Bill his plans for the future, with typical Daley good humor he comes back with a crisp "to keep on with what I'm doing — only to do it bigger and better."

The Opportunity Is Yours

Bill Daley's is admittedly a most unusual case. Not one young person in a thousand starts life the way he did. But the fact that one person has been able to do what Bill Daley did should be a source of inspiration to everyone. If someone in his situation could start making plans for the future to reach as far as he could with that message of love and hope, no excuse can possibly be made for the vast majority of you healthy young people to avoid your responsibility to mankind.

"Go out into the whole world," Christ Himself said. He meant that for every generation. He meant that you also should have a part in carrying His truth and love into the marketplace.

Within each of you there is one thing you possess in common with Bill Daley: love of God and of your neighbor because in each and every human being is the Divine Image. Within each of you, were you to release it, is the capacity to make the whole world a better place than you found it.

There is a big job ahead of you. In the newspapers, in your books and magazines, over radio and TV and in the movies, you have seen and heard how those who deny God are battling to win the world away from Him Who created it. Still, reading and hearing and seeing all this, perhaps you have told yourself: "This doesn't concern me now. When I'm older and out of school or college will be time enough to think about it."

If you have ever thought this, or are thinking it at this moment, you have made or will be making the greatest mistake of your life. You will be leaving the future of your own country in the hands of those who, even now, are being trained to take over your democracy — and the world! — once the opportune moment arrives.

And don't be deceived. These people, many of them students like yourselves, are not merely waiting and hoping for that time to come. They are planning for it now, working toward it now, sacrificing personal pleasure and gain for it now. In a very real sense, these people are missioners, missioners with an evil purpose. They swarm into every phase of national life, particularly into the four great spheres of influence — education, government, labor-management and writing — in the certainty that once they control the thoughts of your nation, they control its destiny.

The Hopeful Side

It's a disturbing situation, yet by no means is it hopeless — far from it. American young people are not anti-religious. Their present-day mistakes come from lack of knowledge rather than from malice or indifference. Indeed, they possess an unusual sense of decency and fair play, not only for all in this country, but for people of all nations. They are more Christian than even they suspect. They are not opposed to Christ. On the contrary, they are actually hungering for His truth. They are waiting for you, their fellow students, to bring Christ to them. But they will not come to you, for they do not know how or why they should do so. You will have to go to them, as Christ commanded you to do.

On the other hand, if you neglect to go and continue going to all people, you will be helping to plunge the world into a nightmare of misery and despair far worse than anything that has ever been witnessed before in history.

God's truth, the very foundation upon which the United States was built, does not belong to you good young people alone. It belongs to everyone. If others have not got it, it is up to you to share your "pearl of great price" with them. A good doctor does not sit in his office during an epidemic, complaining about the state of a community's health, yet doing nothing to relieve the situation. To go back a couple of thousand years, the early Christians did not sit in the catacombs, shaking their heads over the pagan cruelty of the Romans.

Neither should you keep Christ's love and Truth to your-selves. To your fellow students who do not have them, you owe the opportunity of possessing them, also.

That is the one thing which terrifies the godless the world over: the fear that some day all those who believe in Christ will wake up and start acting their beliefs. Once that happens, most of the great problems which plague mankind will disappear overnight.

Living Proof It Can Be Done

There is a saying that imitation is the sincerest form of flattery, and in many respects this is true. Moreover, when such imitation on your part follows the Christopher example of other young people like yourselves who even now are carrying Christ into the marketplace, then it is surely the finest compliment human beings can pay to Him Who made the whole universe and every living creature in it.

More than mere lip service to Truth is needed, however. One young man, whose father is president of one of New York's leading banks, showed what can be done. As a reward for graduating from high school, this youngster was told he could spend the summer vacationing at a Long Island beach. Instead this student, who has picked up a little apostolic spirit all by himself and is an exemplary Christopher, quietly passed up the beach. Unknown to any but a few intimates, he spent each day during the summer in Harlem, caring for thirty-five or forty inner-city youngsters. Of course, he could have given his allowance, but that would have been giving away only money. By giving his time, his thoughts, his solicitude, he gave *himself.* What a change for the better will take place over the world when in small ways and large that one example is multiplied *one million times!* We believe it can be done!

Then there is the story of the young woman who recently graduated from college and set out to get a job. Any kind would suit her, she said, so long as it paid well, didn't require much work, and included a long vacation. On getting what she felt was the ideal position, she wrote us telling us how well off she was. Our reply, sent immediately, was to remind her in a friendly way that she was not only well off but *far off* also. It was a pity, we wrote, that so many wonderful people like her, who could do so much to bring the peace of Christ into the mainstream of American life, were so quickly and inevitably winding up in dead-end streets because they had no thought outside of themselves. And we added that nearly everyone with a crackpot idea was making it his or her business to get into some key spot where they could make everyone else as crazy as themselves.

A few weeks later this same woman wrote us a second letter, and in it was a pleasant surprise! The advice had taken hold and she had just secured another job as assistant to the head of an important department in one of the nation's largest universities. This sudden shift from just a job to a job with a purpose where she was able to exert a far-reaching influence for good among thousands of students was due, as she put it, to the fact that for the first time in her twenty-two years she realized all she had been doing was taking care of herself. Discovering at last that she had an individual, personal responsibility to the rest of mankind, she wasted no time in doing something about it.

After a considerable amount of effort, she surprised herself and everybody else by landing a post at this university. And while she gets less money, works harder, and will have fewer holidays than were in prospect before, yet it is a source of real and deep satisfaction to her to have endless opportunities to be a Christopher — a Christ-bearer — to make the world a bit the better because she is in it.

Each In His Own Way

Another example is that of a young man now completing his graduate work in dramatics at Yale, who came to our office recently to learn about the Christopher idea. His hope, he said, is to establish, or at least help to start, a theater movement in this country along the lines of the Abbey Theater in Ireland. Already he has begun to organize a company which will tour the country and give countless audiences the opportunity of seeing plays truly representative of the best in Christian tradition.

A young woman Christopher, a Catholic college graduate who works for the National Broadcasting Company, told us in a letter: "The idea of being a Christ-bearer is a very appealing one to me. A number of friends here have expressed keen interest in the work of the Christophers. They are in constant contact with the public through writing and broadcasting and therefore can do much good. To discover there are so many people striving for the same goal that I am, of sharing with the general public the truths of Christ, is a comforting and stimulating thought. In my own humble way I am trying to bring Christ to the broadcasting field where He is sorely needed."

One young man, who began his career as an errand boy in the office of an outstanding magazine, is today an important television producer. On his own admission, the thing that spurred him on was the Christopher purpose. Because of that purpose he has reached a position where he is influencing and will continue to influence countless people all over the country.

A senior at the University of California, a young woman with tremendous spirit and initiative, has gone on record with us as pledging herself, upon graduation, to get into some field where she can work just as hard to "save my country and my world as others are in trying to wreck them." And she concludes with: "No matter where or in what capacity I have to begin this job, I'll see it through to the finish."

An author who had several books published before he was thirty states that he is a writer today because as a youngster in the fourth grade of a Chicago public school there had been impressed on his young mind the great good he could do as a writer. "When your first book is published," his teacher told him one day after class, "I want you to be sure and send me a copy." The pupil was only ten years old at the time, yet she pictured his first book as a reality. Twenty years later, it was a reality and the teacher lived to have a copy placed in her hands by the author himself.

At one leading university a group of young men and women have made it their business to get positions on university publications, student councils, and clubs with the view to spreading the Christopher idea and weaving it into every phase of student life. More than this, however, in many cases these self-same young men and women, mindful of the necessity of training others, have sacrificed the honor of actually holding various student posts in order to support and train lower classmen on the way up.

Remember this: the job of preserving freedom is your job, is everybody's job. With faith and love, you can make noble even the lowliest and most hateful occupation. Yet expect ridicule, opposition, and even persecution. But do not cease to try and reach all people, even the most godless and oppressive. After all, it was Christ Himself who said *"Love your enemies, do good to those who hate you, bless those who curse you, and pray for those who persecute you"* (Luke 6:27-28).

The Time Is Now!

Right now, even as students, you can begin to bring Christ to the world in a hundred different ways. Right now, too, you can prepare for the time when you are no longer in school by choosing a career that will enable you to play a vital, personal role in the big job ahead.

Start thinking of your life's work even as you read this. Don't drift into just any job. The godless never make that error. They always get into a position where they can spread their poisonous ideas. Don't take a job, either, just for the salary it pays. Don't be like the West Coast student who, when urged to tell what he planned to do when he finished college, replied, "Gosh, I don't know. Try and get a job and really make some money, I guess. After all, that's what I'm being trained for."

You are not and should not be trained merely to fatten a bank account. You are being trained, or should be trained, to pass along your sound ideas to thousands of other students who will come after you. You may not make your fortune, but you will have the deep satisfaction, for time and for eternity, of knowing that the world, as Bill Daley said, will have been made a little better because you've been in it. All around you, if you look and listen, you will hear talk, talk, talk, and see not enough action.

People are sick of talk about more housing plans, they want houses; they want an end of mere talk about food scarcities, they want food. You who know the Truth and are being trained to be the teachers, the government workers, the backbone of labor, the writers in the communications field, will have to integrate justice into these spheres of influence, so it may go hand in hand with charity.

On every side you will find distractions: promises of better-paying jobs, claims that the profit motive is behind all progress — with no word about your eternal destiny. Ads and other inducements tell you to be selfish, not selfless; to take as much *out* of life and put *in* as little as you possibly can.

Your Goal: To Put In Much

These are not the reasons for which God made you in His Own Image. These are not and should not be the purpose of all your training. God wants each of you to love your neighbor as yourself for love of Him. When you start concerning yourself with all people, you will start to lead a selfless existence. You will start to put into life as much as you humanly can — and take out as little as necessary. Then you will be like the young woman, a sophomore in a Pennsylvania college who, dedicating herself to the distribution of the Christopher idea, wrote:

> …I can do you a service, and myself likewise, by spreading Christian principles and learning to live them myself, thereby becoming a *whole* person, instead of the *half* person that I am.

You will be seeking first things first, and the incidental things second. You will be living "not by bread alone," but *in the love of Christ* which is meant for all mankind. One tremendously inspiring example of man's faith, with the above thought in mind, is contained in the story of Captain Eddie Rickenbacker during the early days of World War II.

In 1942 a small group of men, headed by Rickenbacker, were flying across the Pacific when their plane was forced down at sea. For twenty-three days, from October 21 until their rescue on November 13, they were adrift on life rafts. Hungry, thirsty, exhausted from exposure, and despairing, their hopes were kept alive — by food and water? No! They were sustained by these words of the Man of Galilee, read by Captain Rickenbacker from Private John F. Bartek's GI Bible (Matthew 6:31-33):

"Therefore do not worry, saying, 'What will we eat?' or, 'What will we drink?' or, 'What will we wear?' … your heavenly Father knows that you need all these things.

"But seek first for the kingdom of God, and His righteousness, and all these things will be given to you as well...."

To seven men faced with death, these words from the Gospel according to Matthew were a message of hope, bringing spiritual and mental life-sustaining food.

"Seek first for the kingdom of God...." For each of you students these words have a special significance. In planning your careers, they are the rule by which all your actions have to be governed. Anything less will lead you to exist as only half persons instead of the whole persons God intended you to be.

Your answer to the question, "What was the most important happening in history?" asked not long ago in the *New York Daily News*, will have to be that of fourteen-year-old Brooklyn-born Eddie Kelley. Five other people, all grownups, were asked the question before it came Eddie's turn to speak, and his reply put all five to shame.

"It was the birth of Jesus Christ," he declared enthusiastically. "Christianity is the religion of the countries that rule the world. And Christianity, if we follow its teachings, makes all of us better people. And the world would be ever so much better if all of us would follow the teachings of Christ."

For Eddie there were no doubts, no false illusions about wealth or fame or the thousand and one things which loom on the horizon to distort your mind's vision. He wanted to tell the whole world the most wonderful Truth he possessed. And he succeeded. By a conservative estimate, his words reached at least one million readers of the newspaper in which his statement appeared. At fourteen, Eddie was a practicing Christopher!

Where and When to Begin

Whether you are in grade school, high school or college, you can start right now to be a Christopher.

1. Aim to play an active Christopher part in the world upon finishing your education when you, as a mature person, will be mentally, spiritually and physically equipped to tackle a lifetime job.

2. Meanwhile, start aiming for a definite goal in life, for a pursuit where you will do more than merely earn money. Doing this right away will give you something to live for, something to work toward; in short, you will be going someplace!

3. While in school, you can start building for your future's usefulness — and for your useful future — by:

   a. Praying for the great needs of the world and getting others to pray also.

   b. Developing your writing skill in compositions, letters, articles and the like.

   c. Getting on debating teams, taking an active part in youth meetings, becoming members of school societies — all in themselves excellent training for the future.

   d. Persuading your family, relatives and friends to *vote* and *be informed* on *how* to vote and *why* to vote and *what* to vote for.

   e. Suggesting they take jobs that count.

4. Think frequently and earnestly of the four important fields of

   Education — with a teaching career in mind.

   Government — not only local and state but national administration as well. If you want good government, you will have to take an active, positive part in conducting its affairs.

   Labor — including union activities and management-labor problems as well.

Writing — covering the specialized branches of newspapers, books, magazines, motion pictures, radio and television.

Think, also, of the fields of *social service work* and *libraries.* And some of you think seriously, too, of *religious vocations.* In *all* these fields, the world is won or lost!

5. Avoid the tendency to indulge in flag-waving. Don't belong to a group, project, or society merely to get your name in print or to feel you've done your patriotic best by attending a few meetings. Just as still waters run deep and yeast works quietly in leavening the bread, so what you actually *do*, not *how* you do it, is the thing that counts.

6. Write letters to legislators, newspapers, magazines, radio and television stations. One high school student in Rochester recently made her voice heard in just this way. She wrote her Congressman requesting him to protest against limiting American newspaper reporters in Russia to a mere handful while Soviet newspeople were free to enter the United States in droves. Friends said it was a waste of time, but this student knew Christ wanted everyone to keep trying at all costs. The result? Faith and courage were rewarded in a big way. Not only did the Congressman urge action by our State Department but, under unanimous consent of Congress, the letter was included in the Congressional Record. Not a bad return for a couple of sheets of paper, a little ink and a bit of effort!

By adapting these few suggestions to your individual talents, you will avoid the "fringes" of everyday living. You will be heading instead for the *heart* of the great spheres which influence for better or worse the destiny, not only of your nation, but of your world. And you will be adding to, not subtracting from, the sum total of fine, decent, Christian living.

Take People As They Are

If you would be a good Christopher, however, there are a few additional tips which you would do well to bear in mind.

One of these concerns your approach to young people like yourselves and, later on, to adult men and women with whom you come in contact. To be truly a Christ-bearer, you will always have to accept people not as they ought to be, but as they are. Christ Himself did just that, for He found His followers among folks in all walks of life, in high places and in low. He accepted them all and asked only one thing in return: that they strive to do God's Will.

No matter what the difficulties, get in a spot in life where your influence for good can actually be felt. There is an old saying that "the absent are always wrong." If you are not there, others who would destroy your nation and your world will have that much smoother sailing. The absent never have an opportunity to speak. But by your *living presence* you can bear witness to the Truth.

Have patience. Success as a Christ-bearer is not won over-night. Don't be afraid to *burn* with zeal for spreading Christ's love. Like fire from a furnace, you will warm the hearts of even those who seem to be farthest away from the Truth. The story of a woman in Baltimore bears this fact out. Very much opposed to anything Christian, she found herself strangely moved by the fervor of a young Christopher who made it her business to interest herself in her. "But why ... why trouble yourself about me?" was her question. And the quiet reply came back: "Two thousand years ago Christ died for all of us. The least I can do is to work and love for Him as long as I'm able!"

Keep Plugging Away

Be persevering in everything you do. Take to heart the example of the young man with genuine writing ability who kept plugging away at trying to place his material in the secular publications. Seventeen times he received rejection slips. But on the eighteenth try, he sold a story to a leading magazine — for several hundred dollars!

Retelling this story calls to mind what Stephen Leacock, the eminent Canadian humorist, in his book *How to Write* pointed out. He said that he never succeeded as a writer until he was forty years old, simply because he was afraid of rejection slips. Fear of failure prevented him from making the effort required for success, and his one regret was the number of years he wasted when success might have been his twenty years earlier.

Pray always. For a Christopher to do effective work, prayer is absolutely essential. As a lay apostle you won't get far without it, for you won't be able to give what you don't possess. Without a strong spiritual life of your own, one that is rooted in eternal truths, you will accomplish little for yourself and little for others. There will be an emptiness and shallowness in everything you do without prayer. It is surprising, on the other hand, how your whole activity will be sparked with an ever-deepening faith if only a few minutes are set aside regularly each day for meditation and prayer. Then you will find yourself growing closer and closer to Christ. For you there will be an increasing thrill in the privilege of being a Christopher — a Christ-bearer — of bringing the Prince of Peace into the marketplace.

Pray also, not alone for yourself, your family and your friends, but for the President of the United States, the Congress, the Secretary of State and the United Nations. The test of your sincerity is in what you do for others. The people you do things for are the people you really love. If you say you have love for all men, yet do not reach out to all men, you probably do not have a real, genuine love for them.

Be *missioners* in the true sense of the word. Only in this way will you win the hearts and confidence of everyone.

"The prime requisite of a missioner," a priest writes from Latin America, "is to love his people. That's easier said than done. But there is no getting around it. If the Indians see that we like them, no matter what their faults are, they will gradually open their hearts to us. Once they realize we really want them to come into our homes, and act as they would in their homes, they soon accept us as one of their very own. But that means they must be absolutely free to come at any hour, day or night, often in crowds of twenty or thirty, abounding in all the fragrant odors of an unwashed people.... It gets right down to a literal interpretation of St. Paul's very sound advice of 'becoming all things to all men.' No better formula has ever been found for bringing Christ to men and men to Christ. Every day we see more clearly that our success with the Indians will be in proportion as we do just that."

Your biggest temptation will be to think in terms of "God and myself," to be absorbed in your selfish little world and to leave the running of the big world to those who either hate Christ or know Him not. Even when praying, it is easy to say *"our* Father" and yet mean *"my* Father"; to say *"give us our* daily bread,*"*yet mean "give *me my* daily bread"; to ask God to "forgive *us our* trespasses," and yet mean nothing more than "forgive *me my* trespasses."

All the talk about the brotherhood of man will mean little unless you acknowledge that brotherhood *under the fatherhood of God.* Even from your kindergarten days, always keep that thought uppermost in mind.

So much depends on you young people, you students. Now and for another decade or so, your country carries the great and fearful responsibility of leading the world. On what you do now for Christ, by prayer, by getting others to become Christ-bearers, by going in all the many ways open to you in these years of preparation, and on what you will be doing in the future, hangs a large share of the fate of the world.

Realize and remember that the world is really depending upon *you* far more than you know!

First-Line Christophers

One of the greatest forces for good in Hollywood today — a top-ranking executive of a major film corporation — once studied for the priesthood. After several years training over a quarter of a century ago, however, he realized that God meant his career to be in the world.

Leaving the seminary, he took a job as a busboy in a restaurant in order to earn a living. But he didn't stay a busboy very long. His religious training, curtailed as it was, had aroused in him a longing to reach as many people as he could during his lifetime with the faith and love of Christ that his parents had cultivated within him.

The motion picture field struck him as a particularly fertile sphere since it was already beginning to touch and influence the lives of millions who went to the movies week after week. He didn't stop to ask, "What can I do?" Insignificant as he was then, he was still convinced that by God's grace and his own hard work his power for good could somehow be felt. He began his career at the bottom of the ladder with a small motion picture theater. But menial as the work was, to him it was more than just a job. Into it he carried the high purpose that had motivated his studies for the priesthood.

His strong spiritual values imparted a meaning and a direction to everything he did. His sincere love of God was best reflected in his concern for *everyone* with whom he had contact — even remotely. As anyone with a fixed, broad-visioned goal (whether in itself good or evil) is most likely to forge ahead of those who drift aimlessly without any objective outside of themselves, so he advanced, slowly but surely over the years, from one position to another of still greater influence. Today he is a vital factor in bringing — with but few exceptions — to moviegoers the world over the best in quality screen fare.

In the headquarters office of one of the largest labor unions in the United States there is a young man of the Jewish faith who has devoted the last twelve years of his life to hammering away at the fundamental doctrines of the worker's God-given rights and obligations. In his late thirties now, this man had the desire, as a boy, to be a rabbi. But much thought finally brought him to the realization that such a vocation was not his.

The early consideration of consecrating his life to religion made a lasting impression on him, however. Still imbued with the idea of serving his "neighbor" on more than a material basis, he got a job with a manufacturing concern, joined his local labor union, and set about trying to bring into the union's affairs some concept of spiritual values regarding the dignity of man. Since he first started his work of self-dedication, he has risen to an executive post in this union which represents hundreds of thousands of workers all over the country.

Because of his fixed determination to promote the truth, this Jewish worker has aided greatly in keeping control of his organization in the hands of those who acknowledge the basic relationship of man to God.

Into the Magazine Field

A writer for many nationally known magazines and a contributing editor of one of the most widely circulated monthly periodicals, a man who has won almost unanimous praise for the high quality of his writings, has given as his reason for such quality the time, early in his life, when he actually studied for the Presbyterian ministry. In print (and when he speaks over the radio as well), his whole approach to the problem of everyday living has been in keeping with the purpose which first caused him to begin preparation for the religious life.

At every opportunity he has publicly demonstrated a sound sense of values and high ideals which are even more noticeable in the midst of so much that is cheap and tawdry in the writing profession. What prompted him to discontinue his religious studies is a matter that concerns him alone. Yet in the past twenty-five years he has consciously and actively carried over his "vocation" into the literary field. And rarely has he failed to impress both readers and listeners alike with his strong conviction of spiritual principles.

As Secretary to an Editor

A young woman who thought of becoming a nun finally came to the conclusion that it was not God's Will for her to follow such a life. The first job she took after making up her mind to carve a career for herself in the world was with an airline. The position paid very well, required little mental effort, and provided exceptionally pleasant working conditions. Much to her friends' amazement, however, she wasn't quite satisfied. Upon hearing of the Christopher plan to get large numbers of people with high purpose into the main fields that influence the thoughts and actions of millions, she decided to try for a job which would affect the many, rather than the few.

After several unsuccessful attempts, she finally landed an opening as secretary to the editor of a publishing house. Today, her sense of judgment has come to be valued so highly by her employer that she is frequently consulted for advice in the selection of book manuscripts for publication. She is, therefore, an important factor in determining the kind of material that hundreds of thousands of people will read. Partially at least, she is fulfilling the role of a lay apostle. And because she has realized the great need to have as many as possible go the *full* way and take up the religious life, she has encouraged a friend of hers to become a nun — the vocation she originally thought was to be her own.

Into Labor Relations

In a nationally-listed merchandising concern whose headquarters are in the Midwest, one of the officials in charge of labor relations is a middle-aged man who, as a youth, had his heart set on becoming a lay brother in a religious order. Back in Oregon where he was born he'd been attracted to a life where he could dedicate his entire service to God and to his fellowman. Though he was aware his health wasn't all it should be for such a demanding task, from his sophomore year in high school on through college he'd pursued his studies with this goal in mind.

When he finally made application to enter the order the authorities, after carefully examining his case, reluctantly informed him that while his health, with proper care, might stand up well enough in ordinary life, it might be too frail to bear the never-ending demands of the religious life on his time and energy. Disappointed — but not discouraged — he got on the staff of a West Coast newspaper and stayed there a few years, studying labor relations on the side. What attracted him to this phase of life were its opportunities to improve the lot of large numbers of working people while protecting, at the same time, the just rights of management. Today his influence is felt even outside the concern which employs him. At trade conventions, at labor gatherings, and in the normal conduct of his work in the labor relations field, he has been a tremendous force in bringing Christ into the marketplace of everyday affairs.

These are just five cases out of five hundred that could be mentioned. Yet there must be hundreds of thousands of other Americans like these who have thought at one time or another of dedicating their lives to religion (where there is still need for many more workers) but who for a variety of reasons have not done so. For some it may have been a lack of conviction that such was the right career for them. For others, a condition of health which would require more than usual attention, or insufficient schooling at an advanced age in adult life, or other impediments, minor in themselves, but of sufficient consequence to warrant a decision that the religious life would not be suited to them, or they to it.

In the majority of these cases in which serious thought is given to a professionally religious life, there is, unfortunately, a tendency to lapse back into the crowd once that life, for any reason, proves unattainable. Such individuals often overlook the important service they can render to society if they are determined to do what they can — outside the religious life — to retain and develop the original noble impulse implanted by God, if they are determined to put it to use in some vital way in a profession which, though not in itself religious, abounds in apostolic opportunities.

Those who entertain even a passing inclination towards the religious life are motivated by high and unselfish ideals. There is a willingness to embrace a life requiring constant adaptation to the plans and demands of *others*. Because they are stimulated by such high purpose, these people have disposed themselves to devote the major part of their time and energies to working for *oth-*

ers, with only a small portion of such time and energies set aside for their own convenience and entertainment. They are ready to accept a life of limited income, are ready to put aside the possibility of accumulating even moderate wealth.

For those who have already settled down in life it may be difficult, of course, to transfer to fields of activity where there is great need of apostolic lay action. However, there are tens of thousands of young men and women each year over the country who, though the professional religious life is not for them, would be heartened to know they can still have an important part to play, individually and personally, on a full-time basis.

Since they, above all others, harbor a particular sense of purpose for their lives, they might well be regarded as *first-line Christophers,* carrying into the important spheres of influence a vision and determination which are not always possessed by others.

Snatch Faith From Disaster

Just before his death in 1936, the zealous lay apostle, G.K. Chesterton, made a significant statement that should have a special meaning for every first-line Christopher. He realized far better than most the need for haste in increasing the missioners of light to offset the promoters of darkness. *"The issue is now clear,"* he declared. *"It is between light and darkness, and everyone must choose his side."*

If this issue is faced squarely without any further delay, there is great hope for the future. It concerns all men of good will. Yet it should be expected that those who have felt the call of God at some time or another would be more keenly aware of the peril. It should be expected that they would be more ready and anxious to do something about it and more quickly to be found leaping into the forefront of the ranks of those who are as determined to save the world as others are to wreck it.

In this time of world crisis brought on by advancing inroads of materialism and godlessness, these first-line Christophers have it in their power to snatch faith from disaster, if they can be found in sufficiently large numbers to carry Christ into the marketplace. People like these possess the primary ingredient of purpose — to make God known, better understood, and more widely loved among all people. They recognize that man was born to work and, since God made the world and everyone in it, they further recognize that their first service belongs to Him. In a very real sense they can be God's assistants — Christ-bearers — their lives and their powers not dissipated but utilized in serving Him and all mankind.

If one by one they step forward into the ranks of those who are working for light and not merely talking against darkness, they can do much to change the world itself for the better. The power of just one person such as they cannot be exaggerated, for they hold in their hands the Light of the world, the one Cure for all darkness.

One Small Light

This point was brought home to me quite graphically some time ago at the Metropolitan Opera House in New York. Final arrangements to hold a benefit concert were being discussed, and, at the close of the talks, the assistant manager offered to show me the seating arrangement of the building.

The hour was late and all of the other employees had long since gone. The interior of the auditorium was a blanket of darkness that clouded our view and, as we walked slowly forward, aroused our senses to vague imaginings at the sound of our own footsteps.

Asking me to wait where I was until he could switch on the main lights, the assistant manager left me and went on alone. His figure as he moved down the aisle, then across the stage, could scarcely be seen. Suddenly he stopped. There was the sound of a match scratching against wood. A tiny sliver of light appeared.

Small as it was, from where I stood at the back of the Opera House that speck of light was greater than all the darkness around it. A tiny piece of sulphur-tipped wood had made that possible. After that, to multiply that tiny glow thousands of times and dispel the shadows which still remained, was but the work of a minute. There was the click of a switch. From all corners of the auditorium clusters of electric light flooded the Opera House and the darkness was gone.

That's how it is with all of us. The least person, no matter how insignificant, who is interested in bringing the light of Christ's truth to the whole world is likewise a pinpoint of light in the darkness and is, by God's grace, greater than all the encircling gloom.

All that is needed to remove the rest of the darkness is to multiply that speck of light a million times or more. Darkness disappears in the same proportion as light is added. It is as simple as that. In proportion as Christ-bearers dare to penetrate the darkness with the Light of Christ, so will it diminish and eventually disappear.

Some recognize this challenge. Others do not. One young woman entered the convent and prepared to embrace the religious life, only to realize at the last minute that such a life was not meant for her. Back in the world, she gave up all thought of continuing on as *a part-way* lay apostle. She took a job with the local telephone company where the physical conditions are excellent so far as work was concerned, yet she has neglected to bring with her the spiritual impetus which had once sent her to embrace the religious life.

Another young woman, on the other hand, who also prepared to be a nun, did carry over her high sense of purpose into the world of everyday affairs when circumstances compelled her to give up a cloistered career. A leaflet which described the United

Nations organization and the need for qualified men and women with sound values to work in furthering its aims, gave the cue for which she was searching. In the beginning, however, time after time she was refused employment on the ground that she lacked the proper qualifications. Still she persevered. Finally, she was accepted for a position where she has innumerable opportunities to put Christopher action into practice in helping build a better world.

This woman, as well as a young man who once studied for the ministry in California and is now in charge of an important department of the state government there, together with an ex-seminarian who is the public relations head of a large manufacturing concern which has been free of both management and labor abuses during the entire twenty years he has held that office — each of these and countless others too numerous to mention have brought and still are bringing Christ into the marketplace. All have the same things in common:

1. High ideals and a supernatural purpose.
2. Readiness to embrace a life of self-sacrifice.
3. Recognition of the need for daily spiritual exercises.
4. Willingness to accept cheerfully a life of comparative poverty.
5. Apostolic desire to devote all one's time and effort to bringing God to men and men to God.

We are convinced beyond a shadow of a doubt that many others would plunge into the thick of things if they would just stop to realize the immeasurable good they could do. And there is a breathtaking hope for the future when the thousands of first-line Christophers begin to number in the *hundreds of thousands!*

If You Won't, Who Will?

To have such a lofty life objective — even if only in a passing way — is nothing short of a great gift from God. Even if it cannot be fulfilled completely, it should not therefore be rejected or completely ignored by those who have been so privileged. Perhaps God is calling them to a special apostolate in the world which could never be exercised by one set apart exclusively for the religious life. For as important and necessary as their work is, they cannot go into the many phases of the marketplace. They can guide, direct and encourage, yes; but they depend on lay Christ-bearers to carry the torch into every segment of public life. Those in religious life cannot take a job, for instance, as clerk to a supreme court justice, teacher in a state college, official in a labor union, personnel director in a corporation, staff writer on a newspaper, secretary to a magazine editor, or one of a thousand other posts in vital spheres where so much is at stake.

Any, therefore, who have ever felt stirring within them that divine urge to be another Christ in their own limited way — no matter who they are, where they are, or what they are — should do everything in their power to nurture and strengthen it. If they are generous with God, He will be more than generous with them. If they are willing and determined in His name to go into the turmoil of the marketplace, regardless of how pagan it may be, not to find fault with it but to make it even a tiny bit better because they have added their speck of light — then they will be embarking on a lifetime of thrilling, satisfying, even though hidden, venture that will continue on past death into eternity.

Sink Spiritual Foundations Deep

To do this on a lifetime basis, it is only good sense for them to get into the routine of some sort of spiritual "daily dozen" in order to start sinking their spiritual foundation deep and to keep in good spiritual trim. Doing this will help them persevere over the long years in which they will be vitally needed. It will aid them to overcome paganism before paganism overcomes them. It will assist them to balance "action" with the Source of any good they may do. It will enable them to rise above the trials and temptations that the Devil, with all his subtlety and persistence, always employs to trip up any and all who make things uncomfortable for him. Faithfulness to daily spiritual exercises will serve to keep them ever conscious that they are in the presence of God and that they have a most important mission in life to perform. And they will soon find that their every action becomes a prayer.

It is an old axiom that "you can't give what you haven't got." They should not, however, mistake that to mean that if they are not spiritual experts they can't do anything. No, far from it. There's not a person in the world who cannot give something to the betterment of the world. No matter how far removed from God one may be, he still remains a child of God, and therefore he can still do something for God, thereby coming at least one degree closer to his Maker.

But it is likewise true that one who would play a special role, such as that of a first-line Christopher, must make a special effort to develop his interior life and increase his spiritual power, not simply for his own self-sanctification, but above all else for the sanctification of the world.

The more one prays, the more one grows in the knowledge and love of God, the more hopeful one becomes, and therefore the more effectively brings Him into the world.

For Catholics, the following is offered as a suggested daily schedule:

1. Morning prayers.
2. Meditation or reflection — even three minutes a day would be of value.
3. Whenever possible, attendance at Mass and reception of Holy Communion.
4. Grace at meals, as well as recitation of the Rosary and the Angelus.
5. Reading of a spiritual book (a minimum of five minutes a day) and a few verses of the New Testament.
6. Special prayer to the Holy Spirit before more important tasks.
7. Night prayers and examination of conscience.

This simple routine would take a very small portion of time out of the twenty-four hours a day, but would go a long way in making the entire day purposeful and fruitful.

We Must Not Fail Them

Emphasis on a sturdy spiritual life is necessary above all else, but ranking next in importance is the broad vision of Christ. The Devil takes special delight in getting anyone with apostolic potentialities to become so preoccupied with nooks and corners that he misses the great issues that harass the world. After a while he can't see the forest for the trees. There is strong, gripping temptation to withdraw into one's little world, of getting the "God and myself" complex, instead of the fuller, truer and most essential "God, myself and everybody else" attitude.

It is so easy, strangely enough, for those who devote themselves most faithfully to spiritual exercises to become oversolicitous about saving self, body and soul, while ignoring the pitiful plight of the vast numbers over the earth who are starving — physically, mentally and spiritually. Yes, even those who at one time or other in their lives gave some thought of dedicating themselves one hundred percent to God and souls not infrequently show little hesitancy in taking back about eighty percent when they get into the narrow rut of their own limited spheres.

A special obligation rests on those of us who are Catholics. We are entrusted with the fullness of God's Truth. However, there is always the danger of our overlooking the fact that this Truth of God is meant for others as much as it is meant for us. We have a serious obligation to offer it to them at least by way of good example — but not to force it upon them.

As individuals, we often betray the Truth. Most frequently this betrayal is brought about by failing to have an all-embracing — that is to say, Catholic — desire to bring all people to that fullness of Truth which we are fortunate enough to possess. Yet these others who lack the fullness of the Truth of Christ are by no means all in utter darkness. They, too, possess in varying degrees the true Light Which enlightens every person who comes into the world. They, too, can be bearers of such Light as they possess.

The Gospels make it clear that Christ took men as they were and built on the raw material offered Him. To a chosen few He gave special training and instruction to equip them to be full-fledged, fully accredited apostles. Yet, at the same time, He wished every person who had even the smallest consciousness of His Truth to participate actively in spreading it.

He was willing to accept assistance from any well-meaning source and, in so doing, He occasionally ran counter to His disciples. They were obviously proud of themselves when one day they told Him that a certain man was *"casting out demons in your name, and we tried to stop him, because he doesn't follow with us."* But Christ corrected them: *"Do not stop him; for whoever is not against you is for you"* (Luke 9:49-50). He did not keep His first disciples waiting for years until their instruction would be so perfect that they would be certain not to misrepresent Him. On the contrary, He seems to have urged them to be His messengers from the start, sending them to hand on what Light they had and to publish the good news as they had taken it in.

And those possessed of the Light who carried it to others less fortunate were rewarded by an ever-deepening insight into the Truth in all its fullness and beauty.

So it was then; so it is now. Any effort a man makes to grasp the Truth and live the Life is certain to bring him closer to Christ. *"You would not have sought Me,"* He said to St. Augustine, *"had I not already been seeking you."* God wants man, though He doesn't need him. His grace is penetrating, ever present and ever pressing upon us, and it will use any hold it has on a man to make its grasp more secure. Besides, it is a law of our nature that we can only take in new truth in terms of the old. No missioner begins his work by belittling even the crudest absurdities of the religion of the people to whom he has gone. The good missioner, like St. Paul on the Areopagus, looks for common ground.

Suppose the man with whom you go to work every day believes in some power he is willing to call God. And suppose that some lingering fragrance of the poetry of the Sermon on the Mount still encourages him to believe that God is a Father in heaven Who cares for the birds of the air and the lilies of the field and even one hair on the head of a man. Suppose he has no affiliation with any church and is hardly able to grasp what the word "Christian" means, yet would resent being refused the name. Is he your ally or your enemy?

Perhaps he is a little of both. But you may still urge him to spread that portion of the Truth he already possesses to the many he can contact — and you cannot — who have never heard or imagined that the hairs on their heads meant anything to anyone. If you are thinking to yourself, "Who shall go?" and you feel your friend would answer, "Here I am; send me," why should you hesitate to send him into a darkness more complete than his? By his very going, he may come closer to Christ.

A doctor possessing the truth of medicine does not compromise with disease when he succeeds in getting a sick man to accept only a small portion of that truth. Even getting his patient to follow *one* principle of good health — such as brushing his teeth — is a step in the right direction.

The acceptance of one simple principle, more often than not, arouses a voluntary desire for more, because the human mind has a natural love for truth which sometimes needs but the merest prompting to become more fully aroused. Yet even when the acceptance of a fragment of the truth does not lead to the gradual adoption of the whole, a one percent gain is not to be despised.

In that vein, then, if the millions in our land who belong to no church could be encouraged to embrace and practice even one truth of Christ, they would be advancing, even if ever so slightly, in the right direction.

A Missionary Project

To be an effective apostolic instrument, therefore, a first-line Christopher must be anxious to "go" to all, especially those farthest from Christ, to "launch out" daringly — in short, to be a *missioner.* He should regard the job to be done as plainly *a missionary* project.

God has put that "little bit of the missionary" in every human being. The evil-minded have long recognized this and constantly keep reminding their followers "not to keep to yourselves what we give you, but spread it. Don't take any job. Take a job that counts — a job where you can spread ideas...."

If the missionary vision can spark the evil to action on a world-wide scale never witnessed before, it can be utilized with *far greater effect* for Christ-like work, since that spark was intended by the Creator, not for evil, but for *good.*

For those disposed to aim for the big world in the name of Christ — as He intended they should — the Christopher idea can be a help. It is nothing new; it is as old as the hills. It merely applies to the heart of America the same simple approach used by a missioner in bringing Christ into a pagan city in China.

Instead of sitting self-contained on the city's outskirts, complaining or criticizing, he goes in — again as Christ said to do. Even if he is alone, makes no apparent progress, perhaps is persecuted and even imprisoned, nevertheless he is *there!* He has fulfilled the first thing Our Savior commanded in order for us to win the world, namely, to "go." And because he is there, Christ is working through him, bringing light into darkness, far more than even he realizes.

The Price of Neglect

To neglect all the negative developments in the world any longer is to invite disaster. It will leave the field wide open to those whose only "god" is the collectivist state and who see in man a mere beast of flesh and bone, devoid of an immortal soul. To neglect this task is to allow the "topsoil" of our free society to dry up and be blown away as so much dust.

Such a condition, while desperate, does *not* call for action marked by violence, nor by hysterical outbursts of emotion. Rather does it call for grim, apostolic determination on the part of all Christophers, of first-line Christophers in particular, to work as hard to integrate spiritual values into all phases of life as the enemies of civilization are striving to eliminate them.

If a person needs any special urging to play his or her part as a first-line Christopher and do something to relieve the present tragedy, he or she would do well to reflect for a moment on this possibility: more than a small portion of the world-wide confusion may be due to the fact that people like themselves, who have been given so much spiritually, still hesitate to share even a little of that treasure with those who have nothing at all. That "little," multiplied many times over by others who, like you, hold back, may make all the difference between spiritual life and death for countless millions.

A Rare Opportunity

For all Christophers, first-line lay apostles particularly, there is now an exceptionally rare opportunity to accomplish great things by showing devoted solicitude for the millions in our country who are getting further and further away from the immutable principles of Christ. Communism and other evils may come and go, but this greater problem, involving a gradual loss of appreciation of the main foundations of our civilization, is far more serious than all of them put together. *It is the heart of America's sickness today.* In its wake will inevitably follow a returning paganism, a fading vision, a slow but sure degradation and slipping back to the revolting evils prevalent among mankind before the coming of Christ.

Not for one moment should we overestimate America's position in the world. But we should not underestimate it, either. Whether we like it or not, we in this country have had thrust upon us a terrifying responsibility to show the way to a heartsick world.

It is much more than the dollars, food, medicine and material things of America that the world needs and really wants. What they crave above all else is the spirit that makes America the great nation it is. And that spirit above all else is God's truth proclaiming through the Declaration of Independence, the Constitution and the Bill of Rights that even the least individual, as a child of God, has rights that no man or nation can take from him, the right to life, to liberty, and to the pursuit of happiness which begins here but will have its supreme fulfillment in eternity.

What an honor and a privilege, then, for anyone at this critical time to jump into the breech and help change the course of history. But who is better fitted, better equipped for this than a first-line Christopher? To them it can be said most emphatically and hopefully: *"You can change the face of the world!"*

The Test of Sincerity

It remains to be seen, however, whether they will gladly take up the challenge — or backtrack. There is little danger of exaggerating the important role that they can play, and it will be a terrible pity if they realize this only when it is too late — when they stand before the judgment seat of the Almighty. The test of their sincerity can be fairly accurately measured by how many go into the marketplace, the apostolic vigor they show in seizing the initiative, and in the numbers in which they, as "committees of one," encourage other men and women to be other Christs.

Those who would recapture the daring of Christ and accept His Truth, those who would be other Christs — especially first-line Christophers — can yet take away the play from the godless.

Fired by the missionary spirit God has implanted in them, they can reach for the world as far as they are able. They can seek — whenever and wherever possible — jobs where they can bring into action, on a full time basis, their personal, individual power for the general good. They can influence the many, not merely the few.

They can show the way as lay apostles in bringing the world back to Christ!

CHAPTER FOURTEEN

Speaking in Public

Presentation With a Purpose

The basic rule of public speaking is to know what you want to say and how to say it. A poor speech is usually the result of a failure to meet this fundamental requirement. Every talk must have a definite purpose, must stress some specific point; and the more this purpose is rooted in absolute truth, the greater will be its ring of sincerity. To you, the Christopher, this especially applies.

No matter what the subject, to begin to speak well in public you must be thoroughly imbued with a Christopher purpose. If you are, your very conviction will transmit itself to your listeners and overcome most of the technical speaking flaws you may possess. Secure in the knowledge that Christ works in you and through you who would do His Will, knowing what you want to say and believing in it, having an intense desire to reach as many as possible with the truth which you know, you *will* find a way of properly expressing yourself.

This is not to say, of course, that you will become a gifted orator overnight. The gift of public speech, like so many other gifts, is usually developed, not inherited. Many hours of hard work go into the making of an accomplished speaker. Even the orator from whose lips brilliant phrases just seem to pour has had his moments of open-mouthed silence, the early self-conscious days when he arose to speak and the words refused to come.

Moreover, many a man or woman who is perfectly at ease in across-the-table conversation often becomes very nervous when facing an audience. This happens even to the most seemingly self-assured individuals, yet such nervousness is not altogether a disadvantage.

One man who has been an active public speaker for some twenty-five years, who has taught classes, spoke in Madison Square Garden in New York, and engaged in debates before thousands of people, claims that in the course of a day he averages as many hours on a platform as he does in all his other activities combined. Yet he never goes before an audience without feeling somewhat tense.

"I'm rather grateful for that," he says. "Public speaking requires concentration, very much like hitting a baseball. The batter has to be sharply alert, every muscle and nerve in tight coordination. Likewise, the effective public speaker must feel his body and brain move into high gear."

This moving into "high gear," then, is not something for you to fear. Rather should it be regarded as an advantage, when properly used. The only danger lies in becoming *so* tense that you will not adequately express yourself. If and when this happens, a moment or two of reflection on your role as a Christ-bearer should help to dispel any excessive nervousness. Coupled with this should be a determination to speak in public as often as you can find an opening. The more used you get to the audience and the limelight, the more quickly you will overcome the handicap of stage fright.

From a physical standpoint, nervousness develops from one of three sources:

1. Failure to control your material.
2. Failure to control yourself.
3. Failure to control your audience.

Control of Material

To speak clearly is to think clearly — aloud. It is a mistake to trust to intuition. Who has not had the experience of realizing that there were many important things he should have said and didn't? Think out what you want to say *before* you attempt to say it.

Preparation of material is a prime requisite of successful public speaking. Even in extemporaneous addresses is this true. The best speeches of this kind are usually not as unprepared as they may appear on casual inspection. In most cases they consist of little parts of many speeches a speaker has made in the past. He carries them around in his mind like so many pieces of paper. His extemporaneous genius actually is a job of mental marshaling of data.

Since nearly all good talks are prepared, the method of preparation depends, in part, upon the nature of the speech. If you know, long in advance, that you are to make a speech of a certain length on a specified subject at a definite time, you can do a complete job of preparatory work. You can do research, consult files, gather advice, try out the entire talk on your family or your friends.

On the other hand, if you must speak on the spur of the moment, your problem is somewhat different. You must rely mainly on two things: your brain and your background.

Whenever you are called upon to speak, your brain will have to be alerted quickly to be ready for the task. You will have to decide immediately on the most important point you wish to convey and this decision should be made, if possible, before you get to your feet, *not* afterwards. Once the decision is arrived at, however, follow along that course. *Don't digress,* for not only will your listeners lose the theme of your talk, but you yourself will become increasingly confused. You will become so entangled in a maze of oratorical byways that you will find it ever more difficult to get back on the highway again.

To broaden the scope of your knowledge, reading contributes a fund of information. It is suggested that you use such information in public speaking. The content of your talk should flow from within you, and this is where the Christopher has a particular advantage. He knows the ultimate goal he has to reach; he has a *purpose*. All his persuasion is geared to that end. His chart runs a steady course and is, therefore, that much more sure of success.

If you expect to speak often, you can do a great deal to increase the range of your material. Concentrated research is one method. It is the scholarly approach for those who have the time for intensive study. However, there are many other ways of widening one's background. You might, for instance, develop the habit of clipping out newspaper and magazine articles on a wide variety of subjects which concern you as a *missioner* for *good*. And you will be surprised at how much you gather in a comparatively short time. As a result, you will accomplish a double purpose. You will increase the fund of knowledge held at your fingertips, and you will have a handy reference file in your home.

Occasionally you will hear or read of some incident that might be of value at some later date to illustrate some vital point. Clip out such an item or jot it down. In this connection it is suggested that you purchase from some stationery store both a letter file and a small 3" x 5" card file. Neither of these items need be expensive. The letter file can be used for those pieces of information which run to some detail. The card file can serve to list those references which tell their story in comparatively few words. From time to time, run through your little collection of incidents or anecdotes, discarding those references which are no longer useful. Keeping up to date in this manner is a constant preparation for public speaking that entertains yet conveys a message at the same time.

When you read a piece of good literature, a classic, a famous oration, an important document reprinted in the press, excerpts, perhaps, from the Declaration of Independence, don't hesitate to dwell on the more significant passages. Read them over, again and again — aloud. Soon they will become part of you without your consciously memorizing them. You will absorb thoughts, phrases, and a flow of speech. Both the content and manner of greatness will become part of you.

By no means, of course, is it suggested that you try to imitate anyone. You must be *yourself*, but in so doing you need not hesitate to improve yourself by exposing your eyes, ears and brain to the works of great men and women.

Part of your preparation entails speaking aloud, though not necessarily to an audience. If there is some idea you want to convey, it might be advisable to try it out on your family or on a friend in the course of a casual conversation. This will give you a chance to organize your thoughts into concrete terms. And you will get some inkling of audience reaction.

Make an Outline

In preparing for a talk, an outline is a most suitable device. If the speech is long (fifteen minutes or more), an outline is almost a necessity. If the speech is brief (two to fifteen minutes), an outline is still desirable.

The outline should cover the main points of your address, yet it should not be detailed or you may become more interested in following your outline than in paying attention to your audience. Your outline is your central line of argument, sketched very roughly. It is a reminder of what comes next. It should not be a completely written speech.

Occasionally, of necessity, your outline will go into some detail, as, for example, when you give exact quotations or list statistics and examples. Then it will be perfectly in order to write these items out and even read them to your audience. Your listeners will appreciate such brief interludes, and your speech will gain in authenticity. Christ Himself spoke in parables so as to make His divine truth understood by everyone.

A good talk, like a good story, has a beginning, a middle, and an end. This may sound basic, yet it is a phase of public speaking which requires a good deal of conscious attention. You undoubtedly can recall some speaker who, though he talked at length, just never seemed to get started. Then again, there is the speaker who begins in the middle and stays there. He may talk well and have a good point to convey, but, since he did not prepare the listener by an introduction and sum up his thoughts with a conclusion, more often than not much of what he said is lost. Finally, there is the speaker who starts with the end of his discourse. The audience may know his purpose, yet it will feel indifferent because he failed to develop his points effectively.

Repetition of main points is the hallmark of a well-presented talk. One successful orator offered this formula for a successful speech: "First I tell them what I'm going to tell them," he said. "Then I tell it to them. Then I tell them what I told them." The need to repeat, using different words and examples, is greater in speaking than in writing. A reader can always look back over a printed page; he cannot look back over your words without missing something else you are saying. The spoken word is fleeting. You should state an important idea several times so that your listeners can remember its meaning.

In using your outline, try to stay one step ahead of yourself. As you are finishing one point, take a quick glance at your outline so that your remarks will lead naturally to the next point. This makes for smoother transition and is especially necessary where one point is meant to complement another.

Your speech should be varied in style and illustration, but without real digression. Too much of a sameness, no matter how good in content, will eventually begin to disinterest your listeners.

Preparing a good talk is like preparing a good meal. For the eater, as for the listener, the enjoyment is almost unconscious. But the good cook, like the good orator, knows all about the vast quantity of conscious preparatory work that goes into a meal or a speech. The courses must be planned, the food bought, the tastes balanced, the service neat and attractive. A good talk, like a good meal, begins long in advance of the finished product.

Know Yourself

To know yourself is just as important as to know your material, and often much harder. You can be more objective about material than you can be critical about yourself. Yet knowing one's self is a gentle art, well worth the effort, for in public speaking the audience is constantly making a judgment of you as well as of your material.

The first tendency of a beginner in public speaking is to imitate either real or imaginary characters and try to sound as they do. The effect on the audience is bad. They feel you are not being fair either with them or with yourself.

You are a personality with certain definite qualities of your own. You may be a cool, logical type, not prone to fiery speech, yet you still may be very effective. If you become imbued with the idea that you must increase the emotional content of your talk, you will finish by convincing your audience only of your poor taste. On the contrary, however, you may be essentially an emotional person whose whole tendency is to speak in forceful language. While it may be wise for you to learn some moderation, it would be a distinct mistake for you to force yourself into a pattern of speech unsuited to your temperament. In short, you should fit your style to yourself, gearing the pace of your words to your mental processes.

It is unnecessary to use artificial voice tricks. If you become excited you will shout. If that is your habit, fine. If it isn't, then it is inadvisable to use such an approach when speaking in public. The quality of public speech is not measured by the quantity of sound. A forceful statement, spoken quietly, sincerely, and slowly, can be more powerful than the loudest outburst of words.

Give your points a chance to impress themselves on your listeners. Even if you are a rapid talker, pause after a sentence or a significant passage.

Speak your own sentences, using words with which you are familiar. However, in your spare time you might do well to look up the meaning of new words so that they may become part of your vocabulary. An enlarged vocabulary is like an increased fund of knowledge. It equips you for all kinds of speaking.

Part of knowing yourself is being aware of your bodily movements. An old-fashioned form of public speaking prescribed certain physical gestures to accompany certain expressions. Today this form of speaking is considered out of date. Good gestures are natural gestures. The worst thing you can do is give the audience the impression that you are more concerned with what you do with your hands or feet than with what you are trying to say. After a while your listeners will suspect that the important thing in your public appearance is not your thoughts but your physical extremities. On the other hand, if you forget about your gestures, so will your audience. If you concentrate on what you have to say — and talks with a Christopher purpose are needed urgently — your listeners will reflect your conviction.

Never assume that an audience will be angry at you if you give them a moment or two of silence to allow your words to impress themselves on their consciousness. More often than not, they will be grateful for the opportunity to digest your ideas.

It is a mistake for anyone to begin a talk with an apology. If you are unaccustomed to public speaking, there is no need to advertise the fact. Most audiences will accept you at face value, and, if your words reflect the sincerity of your conviction as a Christ-bearer, then your listeners will accept your message in the same spirit.

Your task, as a speaker, is to impress your motivation on those who hear you. As a Christopher, this should be especially easy since the truth of which you speak has stood the test of time and is rooted in eternity.

Know Your Audience

While all audiences have much in common, they still have their own individual characteristics. To know your audience is to speak more effectively to them. In doing this, there are several factors to be considered.

1. *What is the interest of your listeners?* Not all people are equally interested in the same things. If you know the reason why they have gathered to hear you, you can proceed to use their interest to heighten their concern in your comments. Begin with those things that affect your audience and build on them. It is a sure guide to success.

2. *What is the background of your audience?* In teaching, the instructor speaks in terms of the apperceptive background of his pupils, that is the quantity and quality of background which makes it possible for them to absorb what is being taught in the lesson. Every good speech is comparable to a new lesson. Its point of departure should be the knowledge already in possession of the listeners.

3. *What is the occasion?* Speeches are not always made under the same circumstances. A speech should be adjusted to the mood of the moment. It should be part of the occasion.

4. *What is the size of the audience?* You will not always find it effective to speak to six people as you would to six hundred. Smaller groups demand greater intimacy and informality. Larger groups require a more formal approach. If you know the size of your audience in advance, you will find it easier to prepare to speak to them.

When you have mastered the first three rules of good public speaking — mastery of content, of self, and of audience — there are a few additional suggestions it is well to bear in mind.

Use illustrations. The human mind can follow concrete examples more easily than abstractions. In public speaking it is advisable, as did Christ Himself on numerous occasions, to present illustrations. Explain what you mean by giving an example. Use stories. Retell real incidents. Cite newspaper reports. You will find that you can interest the most apathetic audience with the presentation of even one strong illustration, vividly told.

Look at your audience. This means that you should talk to more than one person among your listeners. Talk to all of your audience, but do not be afraid to pause frequently and look some one person directly in the eye. You will thus get some idea as to how your listeners are reacting to what you are saying. It also makes for audience-contact.

Never become angry with your audience. This is a variation of the Christopher theme of being able to disagree without being disagreeable. No matter how provoked you may be, don't show it. Don't shout; don't lose your temper. Your task as a speaker is to persuade your listeners, to win them over to the God-given truths which form the foundation of your philosophy. If you allow part of your audience, by its behavior, to turn you against the whole group, you have lost and your enemies have won. For a Christopher this point should be especially significant. Sometimes in the group which you are addressing there will be those in whom the idea of a Supreme Being arouses violent hatred. Guiding every action should be the words of Our Savior Himself: *"Love your enemies, do good to those who hate you, bless those who curse you, and pray for those who persecute you"* (Luke 6:27-28).

In the spirit of Christ's love, then, you can go far in reaching the world if you will have the patience and courage to persist in your work of carrying Christ to all people.

CHAPTER FIFTEEN

Reminders for a Christopher

The purpose of this book is to encourage people to restore spiritual values in every sphere, every nook and cranny of American life. The more attention given to these values, the less need will there be for combating erroneous ideas.

But, since it is so easy for all of us, human as we are, to forget the primacy of the spiritual, it is well to be reminded, over and over again, of certain elementary guides and signposts which will help us on the way. In this chapter, then, are set down a few reminders which may be worth a glance from time to time. They are but variations on the triple theme — faith, hope and charity — which it has been the purpose of this whole book to emphasize.

1. Depend more on God, less on self. All of us should pray as if all depended on God and should work as if everything depended on ourselves. Yet we should not forget for one moment that, as St. Paul said, we are not *"competent of ourselves to claim anything as coming from us; our competence is from God"* (2 Corinthians 3:5). The more we realize our strength is rooted in God, the more we will acquire, and be inspired by, an exhilarating assurance that nothing can daunt us… *"For even though I walk through the valley of the shadow of death, I will fear no evil, for You are with me"* (Psalm 23:4).

2. Share the Truth, don't hoard it. One of the easiest ways to keep your faith is to "give it away." On the other hand, one of the surest ways to lose your faith or to weaken it is to keep it to yourself. One thing that stifles peoples' lives and makes their work meaningless is *possessiveness.* It entangles not only the evil and the miserly, but even those who, by their daily actions, seem closest to God. The miser refuses to think of anything but his money and himself. A person can be equally miserly in spiritual things, thinking only of self and God while failing to complete the triangle: (1) God, (2) self, (3) others.

3. Be world-minded, not local-minded. We have a personal responsibility to save the world, not merely to save ourselves and our immediate surroundings. Christ expects us to think and work in terms of helping to bring God to the world, and the world to God. As Americans, we have a special opportunity. Barbara Ward, foreign editor of the *London Economist* and a zealous Christ-bearer in her own right, stated recently: "I believe that the American people — the only people in the world who thought of an ideal first and then built a state around it — will prove in the long run happier, freer, and more creative when they carry that ideal of a free society out into the world, than if they sit at home and hug it to themselves."

4. Go among people; don't avoid them. The Gospels reveal how our Lord was ever on the move, not merely to enjoy Himself but always with the hope and prayer that as He moved among the people, He would reach some who could be reached in no other way. His was the loving purpose of bringing God to men and men to God. He went to dinners, to weddings, to all sorts of gatherings. He engaged in conversation with all types of persons and in all sorts of places — on the roadside, on busy city streets, in village squares, in wheat-fields, at the seashore, at the side of a well, in the desert, on the mountainside — anywhere and everywhere.

And the people flocked to Him because He first went to them: *"I found delight in the sons of men"* (Proverbs 8:31).

Whenever He prayed, He invariably and immediately followed through with some concrete act of love for man. Only as we go among people, however distasteful this may be at times, and though avoiding them might be much the easier course to take, will we truly be Christophers, bearers of Christ. We shall bring Christ's peace and truth to the world in the measure that we imitate His everlasting quest for souls.

5. Push on, don't stand still. "The dogs bark, but the caravan moves on," runs an ancient proverb. We should not feel unduly concerned, therefore, about unfair criticism. We should learn, in fact, to expect it as part of the price of being a follower of One Who pushed on in the face of falsehood, misunderstanding and ingratitude.

6. Aim to serve, not to be served. The noted critic, John Mason Brown, gave vivid testimony to the joy of service in these words: "No one, I am convinced, can be happy who lives only for himself. The joy of living comes from immersion in something that we know to be bigger, better, more enduring and worthier than we are. People, ideas, causes — these offer the one possible escape not merely from selfishness but from the hungers of solitude and the sorrows of aimlessness. *No person is as uninteresting as a person without interests.* The pitiful people are those who in their living elect to be spectators rather than participants, the tragic ones are those sightseers who turn their backs deliberately on the procession. The only true happiness comes from squandering ourselves for a purpose."

7. Be gentle, don't hurt. It's the old, old story which one remarkably keen student of human nature put into words so well: *"You can catch more flies with honey than with vinegar."* It often takes a few more moments and a little added effort to be gentle and considerate, but it pays rich dividends. A hasty, sarcastic word, however, can quickly undo or offset many advances towards good. Seldom is anybody won by being nagged, irritated or belittled. Hurting those most hostile to religion is one sure way of driving them even further away.

8. Submit ideas, don't impose them. Most people resent intrusion, especially in the name of religion. Beware of the attitude of proving you are right and others wrong. On the other hand, however, they are frequently more receptive when truths are *offered* to them, not *forced* down their throats. Christ Himself never intrudes. *"Behold I stand at the door and knock"* (Revelation 3:20), He declared. He is right at the threshold, ever ready, even knocking on the door as a reminder that He is anxiously waiting to help. But He carefully avoids pushing in. He leaves it entirely to each individual to extend the invitation. He builds the fire but He does not strike the match. If Christ Himself is so insistent that cooperation with Him must be entirely voluntary, even at the risk of rejection and denial of Him, a Christopher can be no less considerate.

9. Better to be optimistic than pessimistic. A Christopher, above all others, should stress the hopeful side of things, while still remaining realistic. That people are as good as they are, with so many unsound ideas being spread over the world, is surprising and encouraging. Yet even if things were twice as bad as they are now, there would still be great hope, thanks to God. *"An optimist sees an opportunity in every calamity, a pessimist sees a calamity in every opportunity."*

10. Cheer, don't depress. "No good deed goes unpunished" runs the favorite quip of one zealous Christopher who has had her share of knocks, but who realizes that a sense of humor is one of the best helps in maintaining a sense of proportion. It is a good sign when people are not inclined to laugh at others, but are able to laugh at themselves. To be able to come up smiling in the midst of discouraging obstacles is a great asset for any Christopher. It shows strong faith in God and in others. Those who lack faith in anyone outside themselves tend to be depressed. The forbidding chill of those who are self-centered, rather than God-centered, once caused G.K. Chesterton to remark: *"They do not have the faith and they do not have the fun."* The only ones who are truly gay of heart and ever hopeful are those who are fundamentally spiritual. They know the hidden meaning of St. Paul's words: *"Rejoice in the Lord always; again, I say, rejoice"* (Philippians 4:4).

11. Be more of a "go-giver" than a "go-getter." All of us must have the necessities of life, but we have to be careful lest we favor ourselves too much. We have to be on guard against becoming so preoccupied in securing conveniences and luxuries that we miss the real joy of living — *which is living for others!* Repeatedly Christ said to *"go"* and *"give."* Seldom did He say to *"go"* and *"get."* The example He Himself set and which all people can understand can be summed up in these five words: *"He went about doing good…"* (Acts 10:38). The same should be said of all Christophers.

12. Be daring, not timid. Being bold does not mean being reckless, any more than being timid is a synonym for prudence. Timidity, in fact, is frequently a vice which poses as a virtue. No one in the world should be more daring than a follower of Christ. No one should be willing to risk more, to venture farther. Before them always should be Our Lord's daring challenge to Peter: *"Put out into the deep!"* Peter's first reaction was certainly not one of boldness, but rather one of timid protest. *"Master, we have worked all night long and have caught nothing."* He didn't mention being in the warm, shallow water close to shore where there are few fish to be caught. But then, suddenly stirred by Christ's daring, he quickly added: *"Yet if you say so, I will let down the nets"* (Luke 5:4-5). Taking Christ literally, he did "put out into the deep," into the dangerous waters far from shore. And the result? The nets were so filled with fish that they were breaking, their ships so full that they were almost sinking. Our Lord, immediately after Peter reached shore, added one significant remark to the episode: *"Do not be afraid; from now on you will catch men."* And Peter carried that daring into everything he did for the rest of his life. Those who would be true Christophers will have to be equally daring, avoiding all timidity. If we followers of Christ ever take seriously our Lord's command to "put out into the deep," into the midst of the millions in our land and the billions over the world who are not being reached by anyone in His name, our nets, too, will be breaking. For us, this is a tremendous responsibility!

13. Admit your mistakes, don't deny them. A few years ago, Albert Einstein made a most startling about-face. He publicly acknowledged that the universities and the newspapers that boasted of their everlasting loyalty to truth were failures when the acid test of Nazism came. The only ones who didn't whimper, but who consistently and continually championed the sacred rights of every man, woman and child were those who were definitely for God, not against Him.

"Being a lover of freedom," said Einstein, "when the revolution came to Germany, I looked to the universities to defend it, knowing that they always boasted of their devotion to the cause of truth; but no, the universities immediately were silenced. Then I looked to the great editors of the newspapers whose flaming editorials in days gone by had proclaimed their love of freedom; but they, like the universities, were silenced in a few short weeks....

"Only the Church stood squarely across the path of Hitler's campaign for suppressing truth. I never had any special interest in the Church before, but now I feel a great affection and admiration because the Church alone had had the courage and persistence to stand for intellectual truth and moral freedom. I am forced thus to confess that what I once despised I now praise unreservedly."

By admitting his mistake, Einstein accomplished a great deal of good. He brought to the attention of millions a truth which they might otherwise never have known. To acknowledge one's errors is humiliating, but it is often through humiliations, willingly endured, that we deepen and strengthen our spiritual roots.

14. *Be humble, not proud.* Most of us get into one sort of trouble or another because we try to fool ourselves. There is the everlasting temptation to pretend to be something we are not. So many headaches can be avoided by following the simple advice: *"Be yourself!"* If God gives us only one talent, He wants us to use it efficiently, but He certainly does not wish us to try to fool the public, to give the impression that we have five or ten talents. Of a young businessman who had unusual success, despite certain limitations, someone wisely said, *"He is smart enough to know what he doesn't know."* Pride can trip up any of us. It is the most insidious of sins. It reaches into the most protected and sacred spheres. It is the Devil's Number One Specialty. *"I will not serve!"* said Lucifer. And *"by that sin the angels fell."* Pride will react on us in proportion as we exaggerate self and overlook the fact that anything and everything we have, little or much, comes from God.

15. *Inspire confidence, don't dishearten.* "There is no surprise more magical than the surprise of being loved," Charles Morgan once said. "It is God's finger on a man's shoulder." There's a bit of nobility in the worst of human beings because all are made in God's image and that image can never be completely effaced or lost. Never write anybody off! There's always hope! Even the man who has decided to have nothing whatever to do with God isn't frozen in that state of mind. Deep in the very roots of his being, and just because he is created in the Divine Image, there is an ever-present tug toward God. It is the privilege of Christophers to help him become aware of this tremendous tug. For this very reason, that in the very being of every person there is a pull toward God, Christophers can honestly say to anyone, with little danger of hurting his or her feelings, "There's a lot of good in you!" They

can inspire confidence by a word or by a friendly glance. After all, this is a part of that greatest virtue of charity. And for a definition of charity, someone once offered:

It's silence when your words would hurt.
It's patience when your neighbor's curt.
It's deafness when a scandal flows.
It's thoughtfulness for others' woes.
It's promptness when stern duty calls.
It's courage when misfortune falls.

16. Disagree without being disagreeable. A child, who had spent quite a bit of extra time at her prayers one particular evening and had been questioned by her mother as to the reason, replied: "I was praying that all bad people would be good, and all good people nice!" One of the greatest injuries to religion comes from a few of its most loyal adherents who are correct in all matters, *save one.* They persist in being disagreeable when it would be just as easy to remain agreeable, even while differing. If they realized how that slightly sour note has a big effect in keeping large numbers away from religion, many would undoubtedly change to a more pleasant attitude without delay. It is most important for a Christopher to be *pleasantly* firm when it is necessary to be firm. But being disagreeable is a sign of weakness.

17. See both points of view, not merely your own. An anonymous author sums up this point as follows:

"When the other fellow acts that way, he's *ugly*;
When you do it, it's *nerves.*
When he's set in his ways, he's *obstinate*;
When you are, it's just *firmness.*
When he doesn't like your friends, he's *prejudiced*;
When you don't like his, you are *simply showing good judgment of human nature.*
When he tries to be accommodating, he's *polishing the apple*;

When you do it, you're using *tact.*
When he takes time to do things, he *is dead slow;*
When you take ages, you are *deliberate.*
When he picks flaws, he's *cranky;*
When you do, you're *discriminating.*"

18. Be patient, not impetuous. There is little danger of making a mistake by proceeding gently, patiently, though persistently. But much harm can result from being unpleasantly brusque. Consider: "Why were the saints saints? Because they were cheerful when it was difficult to be cheerful, patient when it was difficult to be patient; and because they pushed on when they wanted to stand still, and kept silent when they wanted to talk, and they were agreeable when they wanted to be disagreeable. That was all. It was quite simple and always will be."

19. Be a doer, not just a talker. A frequent inmate of the county jail in a small Midwest community has for his motto, "Death before dishonor." Writing it down on a piece of paper wasn't enough for him. He had it *tattooed on his arm!* To him can be applied the question frequently on the lips of a skeptic: "Do you talk and *do,* or do you only *talk?*" This skeptic would always explain that he had heard many enthusiasts talk about the great things they planned to do. But, he complained, they never got past the talking stage.

This danger has been eloquently expressed by C. S. Lewis' devil in *The Screwtape Letters* as he refers to his effort to tempt the good man: "The great thing is to prevent his doing anything. As long as he does not convert it into action, it does not matter how much he thinks about this new repentance. Let the brute wallow in it ... The more often he feels without acting, the less he will ever be able to act, and, in the long run, the less he will be able to feel."

Talk without performance is evidence of lack of sincerity:

"Just as the body without the spirit is dead, so faith without works is also dead" (James 2:26).

One of the easiest ways to *be* good is to *do* good.

20. Don't flee suffering; use it. At the recent *Life* Round Table on the *Pursuit of Happiness,* a panel of eighteen men and women spent fifteen hours discussing the third right to be enumerated in the Declaration of Independence. Of the distinguished group selected for this panel, no one did more to emphasize spiritual values than a young woman, Betsy Barton, who lost the use of both legs fourteen years earlier in an automobile crash.

In closing, Miss Barton said: "It is my experience that suffering and pain are, unfortunately, the great character-builders — not that suffering is good in itself, but because it often helps to shift our expectation of happiness from without to a search for it from within.... Mystics have shown us that when they set out to achieve spiritual understanding, they cleared the way by depriving themselves of *things,* by their own will. But we are so suffocated with things and with distractions that the real pursuit of happiness is almost impossible.... I feel that we should learn how not to be afraid of being alone. Then we would not seek to run from aloneness into distractions. If self-understanding is a component of happiness (as we agreed) this is best achieved in silence, in stillness and in solitude.... Happiness is primarily an inner state, an inner achievement. In other words, I would like to close by saying that the Kingdom of Heaven is within us."

As Betsy Barton pointed out, suffering may be the means whereby we achieve self-understanding. And it is in the measure that we achieve self-understanding that we are able to reach out with understanding to others. Happiness is not to be found in the pursuit of *things,* nor in the possession of *things.* It comes as a by-product of *living* and *giving,* of suffering and participation in the sufferings of others. *"It is through many tribulations that we must enter the kingdom of God"* (Acts 14:22).

21. Keep first things first. Our Lord over and over again stressed we should do *first* what most of us by nature are inclined to do *last*. He didn't say, for instance: "Love yourself and then if it isn't too much bother, take an interest in the welfare of others." He put it just the other way — and He made it crystal-clear: *"Love your neighbor."* How much? *"As yourself!"*

He could have urged us to be "simple as doves and wise as serpents." But here again He specified first the quality that presumes being on one's toes: *"Be as wise as serpents and as simple as doves"* (Matthew 10:16). As things now stand, most good people are "simple as doves," which requires little effort, where most of those who are bent on evil are "wise as serpents." Once there are found enough followers of Christ who strive to combine both qualities, then great things are bound to happen.

And, again, Christ did *not* say: "Go into the byways and the highways." He purposely put the more important and the least likely first: *"Go into the highways and the byways."* Christians at present are largely confining themselves to the "byways." Those who are striving relentlessly to destroy the world and enslave mankind concentrate almost entirely on the "highways." They know that once they control the main spheres of influence (education, government, labor-management, the writing field) they automatically control the "byways" as well. It isn't hard to understand, therefore, why the Christopher objective lays special stress on (a) *"Love your neighbor,"* (b) *"Be as wise as serpents,"* and (c) *"Go into the highways."*

CHAPTER SIXTEEN

Christ Speaks to You

Nothing could be more fitting than that Our Lord should have the last word. So, in this final chapter, Christ Himself speaks to you, His Christ-bearer, in His own words.

His Claim to Be Heard

1. "The Father and I are one." (John 10:30)
2. "Very truly, I say to you, before Abraham came to be, I am." (John 8:58)
3. "I am the Way, and the Truth, and the Life. No one comes to the Father except through Me." (John 14:6)
4. "Heaven and earth will pass away, but My words will not pass away." (Matthew 24:35)
5. "For this I was born, and for this I came into the world, to bear witness to the truth. Everyone who is of the truth listens to My voice." (John 18:37)
6. "I am the light of the world. Whoever follows Me will never walk in darkness but will have the light of life." (John 8:12)
7. "And this is eternal life, that they may know You, the only true God, and Jesus Christ Whom You have sent." (John 17:3)

8. "I am the resurrection and the life. Those who believe in Me, even though they die, will live." (John 11:25)

9. "I am the vine, you are the branches. Those who abide in Me and I in them bear much fruit, because apart from Me you can do nothing." (John 15:5)

10. "Every plant that My heavenly Father has not planted will be uprooted." (Matthew 15:13)

11. "Blessed are you, Simon son of Jonah! For flesh and blood has not revealed this to you, but My Father in heaven. And I tell you, you are Peter, and on this rock I will build My church, and the gates of hell will not prevail against it. I will give you the keys of the kingdom of heaven, and whatever you bind on earth will be bound in heaven, and whatever you loose on earth will be loosed in heaven." (Matthew 16:17-19)

12. "The one who falls on this stone will be broken to pieces; and it will crush anyone on whom it falls." (Matthew 21:44)

13. "I am the gate. Whoever enters by Me will be saved." (John 10:9)

14. "I am the bread of life. Whoever comes to Me will never be hungry, and whoever believes in Me will never be thirsty." (John 6:35)

15. "Those who eat My flesh and drink My blood have eternal life, and I will raise them up on the last day, for My flesh is true food and My blood is true drink. Those who eat My flesh and drink My blood abide in me, and I in them. Just as the living Father sent Me, and I live because of the Father, so whoever eats Me will live because of Me." (John 6:54-57)

The Commission to Go

16. "All authority in heaven and on earth has been given to Me. Go therefore and make disciples of all nations, baptizing them in the name of the Father and of the Son and of the Holy Spirit,

and teaching them to obey everything that I have commanded you. And remember, I am with you always, to the end of the age." (Matthew 28:18-20)

17. "Go into all the world and proclaim the good news to the whole creation. The one who believes and is baptized will be saved; but the one who does not believe will be condemned." (Mark 16:15-16)

18. "As the Father has sent Me, so I send you." (John 20:21)

19. "You did not choose Me but I chose you. And I appointed you to go and bear fruit, fruit that will last." (John 15:16)

20. "The harvest is plentiful, but the laborers are few; therefore ask the Lord of the harvest to send out laborers into His harvest." (Matthew 9:37-38)

21. "I have other sheep that do not belong to this fold. I must bring them also, and they will listen to My voice. So there will be one flock, one shepherd." (John 10:16)

22. "Follow Me, and I will make you fishers of men." (Matthew 4:19)

23. "Put out into the deep water and let down your nets for a catch." (Luke 5:4)

24. "Do not be afraid; from now on you will catch men." (Luke 5:10)

25. "See, I am sending you out like sheep into the midst of wolves; so be wise as serpents and innocent as doves." (Matthew 10:16)

26. "Let us go on to the neighboring towns, so that I may proclaim the message there also, for that is what I came to do." (Mark 1:38)

27. "My Father is glorified by this, that you bear much fruit and become My disciples." (John 15:8)

28. "You are the light of the world. A city built on a hill cannot be hid. No one after lighting a lamp puts it under the bushel basket, but on the lamp stand, and it gives light to all in the house. In the same way, let your light shine before others, so that they

may see your good works and give glory to your Father in heaven."
(Matthew 5:14-16)

29. "And everyone who has left houses or brothers or sisters
or father or mother or children or fields, for My name's sake, will
receive a hundredfold, and will inherit eternal life." (Matthew
19:29)

By Means of Love

30. "'You shall love the Lord your God with all your heart,
and with all your soul, and with all your mind.' This is the greatest and first commandment. And a second is like it: 'You shall love
your neighbor as yourself.' On these two commandments hang all
the law and the prophets." (Matthew 22:37-40)

31. "I give you a new commandment, that you love one another. Just as I have loved you, you also should love one another."
(John 13:34)

32. "This is My commandment, that you love one another
as I have loved you." (John 15:12)

33. "By this everyone will know that you are My disciples, if
you have love for one another." (John 13:35)

34. "No one has greater love than this, to lay down one's life
for one's friends." (John 15:13)

35. "You are My friends if you do what I command you."
(John 15:14)

36. "For the Son of Man came not to be served but to serve,
and to give His life as a ransom for many." (Mark 10:45)

37. "You have heard that it was said, 'You shall love your
neighbor and hate your enemy.' But I say to you, Love your enemies and pray for those who persecute you, so that you may be
children of your Father in heaven, for He makes the sun rise on
the evil and on the good, and sends rain on the righteous and on
the unrighteous." (Matthew 5:43-45)

38. "For if you love those who love you, what reward do you have? Do not even the tax collectors do the same? And if you greet only your brothers and sisters, what more are you doing than others? Do not even the Gentiles do the same?" (Matthew 5:46-47)

39. "Truly I tell you, insofar as you did it to one of the least of these brothers, you did it to Me." (Matthew 25:40)

40. "Do you see this woman? I entered your house; you gave Me no water for My feet, but she has bathed My feet with her tears and dried them with her hair. You gave Me no kiss, but from the time I came in she has not stopped kissing My feet. You did not anoint My head with oil, but she has anointed My feet with ointment. Therefore, I tell you, her sins, which were many, have been forgiven; hence she has shown great love. But the one to whom little is forgiven, loves little." (Luke 7:44-47)

41. "Truly I tell you, this poor widow has put in more than all those who are contributing to the treasury. For all of them have contributed out of their abundance; but she out of poverty has put in everything she had, all she had to live on." (Mark 12:43-44)

42. "Father, forgive them; for they do not know what they are doing." (Luke 23:34)

43. "Those who are well have no need of a physician, but those who are sick. Go and learn what this means, 'I desire mercy, not sacrifice.' For I have come to call not the righteous but sinners." (Mt 9:12-13)

44. "The Son of Man came to seek out and to save the lost." (Luke 19:10)

45. "God did not send the Son into the world to condemn the world, but in order that the world might be saved through Him." (John 3:17)

46. "There will be more joy in heaven over one sinner who repents than over ninety-nine righteous persons who need no repentance." (Luke 15:10)

47. "So it is not the will of your Father in heaven that one of these little ones should be lost." (Matthew 18:14)

48. "He will not break a bruised reed or quench a smoldering wick until He brings justice to victory." (Matthew 12:20)

49. "For John the Baptist has come eating no bread and drinking no wine, and you say, 'He has a demon'; the Son of Man has come eating and drinking, and you say, 'Look, a glutton and a drunkard, a friend of tax collectors and sinners!'" (Luke 7:33-34)

50. "Woman, where are they? Has no one condemned you?" She said, "No one, sir." And Jesus said, "Neither do I condemn you. Go your way, and from now on do not sin again." (John 8:10-11)

51. "'Bring out a robe — the best one — and put it on him; put a ring on his finger and sandals on his feet. And get the fatted calf and kill it, and let us eat and celebrate; for this son of mine was dead and is alive again; he was lost and is found!' And they began to celebrate." (Luke 15:22-24)

The Gain of Suffering

52. "Remember the word that I said to you, 'Servants are not greater than their master.' If they persecuted Me, they will persecute you; if they kept My word, they will keep yours also." (John 15:20)

53. "If the world hates you, be aware that it hated Me before it hated you." (John 15:18)

54. "I have given them Your word, and the world has hated them because they do not belong to the world, just as I do not belong to the world. I am not asking You to take them out of the world, but I ask You to protect them from the evil one." (John 17:14-15)

55. "Very truly, I tell you, you will weep and mourn, but the world will rejoice; you will have pain, but your pain will turn into joy. When a woman is in labor, she has pain, because her hour

has come. But when her child is born, she no longer remembers the anguish because of the joy of having brought a human being into the world. So you have pain now; but I will see you again, and your hearts will rejoice, and no one will take your joy from you." (John 16:20-22)

56. "Then they will hand you over to be tortured and will put you to death, and you will be hated by all nations because of My name. Then many will fall away, and they will betray one another and hate one another." (Matthew 24:9-10)

57. "I have said this to you, so that in Me you may have peace. In the world you face persecution. But take courage; I have conquered the world!" (John 16:33)

58. "Those who love their life lose it, and those who hate their life in this world will keep it for eternal life." (John 12:25).

59. "If any want to become My followers, let them deny themselves and take up their cross daily and follow Me." (Luke 9:23)

60. "Those who find their life will lose it, and those who lose their life for My sake will find it." (Matthew 10:39)

61. "Very truly, I tell you, unless a grain of wheat falls into the earth and dies, it remains just a single grain; but if it dies, it bears much fruit." (John 12:24)

62. "If your right eye causes you to sin, tear it out and throw it away; it is better for you to lose one of your members than for your whole body to be thrown into hell." (Matthew 5:29)

63. "The kingdom of heaven has suffered violence, and the violent take it by force." (Matthew 11:12)

64. "You have heard that it was said, 'You shall not commit adultery.' But I say to you that everyone who looks at a woman with lust has already committed adultery with her in his heart." (Matthew 5:27-28)

65. "Blessed are the pure in heart, for they will see God." (Matthew 5:8)

66. "Blessed are the poor in spirit, for theirs is the kingdom of heaven." (Matthew 5:3)

67. "Blessed are those who hunger and thirst for righteousness, for they will be filled." (Matthew 5:6)

68. "Blessed are those who are persecuted for righteousness' sake, for theirs is the kingdom of heaven." (Matthew 5:10)

69. "Blessed are you when people revile you and persecute you and utter all kinds of evil against you falsely on My account. Rejoice and be glad, for your reward is great in heaven, for in the same way they persecuted the prophets who were before you." (Matthew 5:11-12)

70. "Do not fear those who kill the body but cannot kill the soul; rather fear Him Who can destroy both soul and body in hell." (Matthew 10:28)

71. "But the one who endures to the end will be saved." (Matthew 24:13)

72. "Come to Me, all you who are weary and carrying heavy burdens, and I will give you rest. Take My yoke upon you, and learn from Me; for I am gentle and humble in heart, and you will find rest for your souls. For My yoke is easy, and My burden is light." (Matthew 11:28-30)

73. "Repent, for the kingdom of heaven has come near." (Matthew 4:17)

74. "This kind can come out only through prayer." (Mark 9:28)

75. "Get behind Me, Satan! You are a stumbling block to Me; for you are setting your mind not on divine things, but on human things." (Matthew 16:23)

76. "No one can serve two masters; for a slave will either hate the one and love the other, or be devoted to the one and despise the other. You cannot serve both God and mammon." (Matthew 6:24)

The Final Accounting

77. "Do not let your hearts be troubled. Believe in God, believe also in Me. In My Father's house there are many dwelling places. If it were not so, would I have told you that I go to prepare a place for you?" (John 14:1-2)

78. "For God so loved the world that He gave His only Son, so that everyone who believes in Him may not perish but may have eternal life." (John 3:16)

79. "For the Son of Man is to come with His angels in the glory of His Father, and then He will repay everyone for what has been done." (Matthew 16:27)

80. "Everyone therefore who acknowledges Me before others, I also will acknowledge before My Father in heaven; but whoever denies Me before others, I will also deny before My Father in heaven." (Matthew 10:32-33)

81. "Do not lay up for yourselves treasures on earth, where moth and rust consume and where thieves break in and steal, but lay up for yourselves treasures in heaven, where neither moth nor rust consumes and where thieves do not break in and steal. For where your treasure is, there will your heart be also." (Matthew 6:19-20)

82. "Look at the birds of the air: they neither sow nor reap nor gather into barns, and yet your heavenly Father feeds them. Are you not of more value than they?" (Matthew 16:26)

83. "When you give a dinner or a banquet, do not invite your friends or your brothers or your kinsmen or rich neighbors, lest they also invite you in return, and you be repaid. But when you give a feast, invite the poor, the maimed, the lame, the blind, and you will be blessed, because they cannot repay you. You will be repaid at the resurrection of the just." (Luke 14:12-14)

84. "A man once gave a great banquet, and invited many; and at the time for the banquet he sent his servant to say to those who had been invited, 'Come; for all is now ready.' But they all

alike began to make excuses. The first said to him, 'I have bought a field, and I must go out and see it; I pray you, have me excused.' And another said, 'I have bought five yoke of oxen, and I go to examine them; I pray you, have me excused.' And another said, 'I have married a wife, and therefore I cannot come.' So the servant came and reported this to his master. Then the householder in anger said to his servant, 'Go out quickly to the streets and lanes of the city, and bring in the poor and maimed and blind and lame.'" (Luke 12:16-21)

85. "There was a rich man who had a steward, and charges were brought to him that this man was wasting his goods. And he called him and said to him, 'What is this that I hear about you? Turn in the account of your stewardship, for you can no longer be steward.'" (Luke 16:2)

86. "Then He will say to those on His left hand, 'Depart from Me, you cursed, into the eternal fire prepared for the devil and his angels.'" (Matthew 25:41)

87. "Then the King will say to those at His right hand, 'Come, O blessed of My Father, inherit the kingdom prepared for you from the foundation of the world.'" (Matthew 25:34)

ST PAULS

This book was produced by St. Pauls/Alba House, the Society of St. Paul, an international religious congregation of priests and brothers dedicated to serving the Church through the communications media.

For information regarding this and associated ministries of the Pauline Family of Congregations, write to the Vocation Director, Society of St. Paul, P.O. Box 189, 9531 Akron-Canfield Road, Canfield, Ohio 44406-0189. Phone (330) 702-0396; or E-mail: spvocationoffice@aol.com or check our internet site, www.albahouse.org

Index

Notes

The Author

The author at cairn on summit of southernmost Pharaoh Peak; Mt. Ball in distance on left.

Mike Potter first hiked in Banff National Park in 1970 and knows it intimately, from towering peaks to tiny hummingbirds.

From 1983 to 1996, Mike worked as an interpretive naturalist with Parks Canada, leading guided walks and presenting evening programs to park visitors.

Mike has written five other books published by Luminous Compositions, including the companion to this volume: **Hiking Lake Louise** (revised edition, 1999).

His other titles include **Central Rockies Wildflowers** (1996), **Central Rockies Placenames** (1997), **Fire Lookout Hikes in the Canadian Rockies** (1998), and **Ridgewalks in the Canadian Rockies** (2001).

Mike contributed the first of his "Backcountry Banff" columns, from which this book evolved, to the *Banff Crag & Canyon* newspaper in 1987.

He finds inspiration and rejuvenation in his outdoor experiences, and shares with Edward Abbey the conviction that "wilderness is not a luxury but a necessity of the human spirit, and as vital to our lives as water and good bread."